OpenStack Sahara Essentials

Integrate, deploy, rapidly configure, and successfully manage your own big data-intensive clusters in the cloud using OpenStack Sahara

Omar Khedher

PUBLISHING

BIRMINGHAM - MUMBAI

OpenStack Sahara Essentials

First published: April 2016

Production reference: 1200416

Published by Packt Publishing Ltd.
Livery Place
35 Livery Street
Birmingham B3 2PB, UK.

ISBN 978-1-78588-596-9

www.packtpub.com

Credits

Author
Omar Khedher

Reviewer
Ami Shmueli

Acquisition Editor
Nitin Dasan

Content Development Editor
Abhishek Jadhav

Technical Editor
Nirant Carvalho

Copy Editors
Madhusudan Uchil
Jonathan Todd

Project Coordinator
Judie Jose

Proofreader
Safis Editing

Indexer
Priya Sane

Graphics
Kirk D'Penha

Production Coordinator
Shantanu N. Zagade

Cover Work
Shantanu N. Zagade

About the Author

Omar Khedher is a systems and network engineer. He worked for a few years in cloud computing environments and was involved in several private cloud projects based on OpenStack. Leveraging his skills as a system administrator in virtualisation, storage, and networking, he works as cloud system engineer for a leading advertising technology company, Fyber, based in Berlin. Currently, together with several highly skilled professional teams in the market, they collaborate to build a high scalable infrastructure based on the cloud platform.

Omar is also the author of another OpenStack book, *Mastering OpenStack*, *Packt Publishing*. He has authored also few academic publications based on new researches for the cloud performance improvement.

I would like to dedicate this book to my lovely parents, my brothers, and my dear 'schat', who have supported me remotely throughout the writing of this book. Big thanks go out to my PhD supervisor Dr. Mohamed in KSA, to my professional friend Andre Van De Water , to Belgacem in Tunisia for their guidance and critique and to my colleagues at Fyber for sharing knowledge. I extend a special thanks to Kenji Shioda for providing resources in his cloud platform to make the book labs happen. I would like to thank all the reviewers of this book for their accurate notices and precious remarks. A thank you to Abhishek Jadhav for the continued and great work on this book, which has taken a good piece of work. And with no doubt, a great thanks to the immense work provided by the OpenStack community to deliver such an amazing project, Sahara, that empowers the OpenStack journey.

About the Reviewer

Ami Shmueli has 18 years of experience in IT, System, DevOps, Automation.

He fulfilled different roles over those years as Infrastructure manager, Technical product manager, DevOps leader, and other technical and managerial roles.

He has vast experience in cloud design and architecture for telco enterprises and financial companies.

Ami has a proven experience in both R&D and infrastructure domains. Currently, Ami is involved in building high-scale on-premise clouds based on OpenStack as well as leading several application modernization projects on top of AWS, Azure, and SoftLayer.

www.PacktPub.com

eBooks, discount offers, and more

Did you know that Packt offers eBook versions of every book published, with PDF and ePub files available? You can upgrade to the eBook version at www.PacktPub.com and as a print book customer, you are entitled to a discount on the eBook copy. Get in touch with us at customercare@packtpub.com for more details.

At www.PacktPub.com, you can also read a collection of free technical articles, sign up for a range of free newsletters and receive exclusive discounts and offers on Packt books and eBooks.

https://www2.packtpub.com/books/subscription/packtlib

Do you need instant solutions to your IT questions? PacktLib is Packt's online digital book library. Here, you can search, access, and read Packt's entire library of books.

Why subscribe?

- Fully searchable across every book published by Packt
- Copy and paste, print, and bookmark content
- On demand and accessible via a web browser

Table of Contents

Preface

OpenStack, the ultimate cloud computing operating system, keeps growing and gaining more popularity around the globe. One of the main reasons of OpenStack's success is the collaboration of several big enterprises and companies worldwide. Within every new release, the OpenStack community brings a new incubated project to the cloud computing open source world. Lately, big data has also taken a very important role in the OpenStack journey. Within its broad definition of the complexity of data management and its value extraction, the big-data business faces several challenges that need to be tackled. With the growth of the concept of cloud paradigm in the last decade, the big-data world can also be offered as a service. Specifically, the OpenStack community has taken on such a challenge to turn it into a very unique opportunity: Big Data as a Service. The Sahara project makes provisioning a complete elastic Hadoop cluster a very seamless operation with no need for touching the underlying infrastructure. Running on OpenStack, Sahara becomes a very mature project that supports Hadoop and Spark, the open source in-memory computing framework. That becomes a very good deal to find a parallel world about Big Data and Data Processing in Sahara named Elastic Data Processing. Sahara, formerly known as Savanna, has become a very attractive project, mature and supporting several big data providers.

In this book, we will explore the main motivation of using Sahara and how it interacts with other services of OpenStack. The main motivation of using Sahara is the facilities exposed from a central dashboard to manage big-data infrastructure and simplify data-processing tasks. We will walk through the installation and integration of Sahara OpenStack, launch clusters, execute sample jobs, explore more functions, and troubleshoot some common errors. By the end of this book, you should not only understand how Sahara operates and functions within the OpenStack ecosystem but also realize its major use cases of cluster and workload management.

What this book covers

Chapter 1, The Essence of Big Data in the Cloud, introduces the motivation of using the cloud computing paradigm in big-data management. The chapter will focus on the need of a different way to resolve big-data analysis complexity by looking at the Sahara project and its internal architectural design.

Chapter 2, Integrating OpenStack Sahara, walks through all the necessary steps for installing a multi-node OpenStack environment and integrating Sahara, and it shows you how to run it successfully along with the existing OpenStack environment.

Chapter 3, Using OpenStack Sahara, describes the workflow of Hadoop cluster creation using Sahara. The chapter shows you how to speed up launching clusters using templates through Horizon and via the command line in OpenStack.

Chapter 4, Executing Jobs with Sahara, focuses on executing sample jobs for elastic data processing based on the example in the previous chapter using Sahara. It also gives you the opportunity to execute jobs using the Sahara REST API and shows what is going on under the hood from the API's call level in OpenStack.

Chapter 5, Discovering Advanced Features with Sahara, dives into more advanced Sahara functionalities, such as anti-affinity and data-locality concepts. This chapter also covers the different supported plugins existing in Sahara and tells you why you need each of them. In addition, you will learn how to customize the Sahara setup based on several storage and network configurations in the OpenStack environment.

Chapter 6, Hadoop High Availability Using Sahara, discusses building a highly available Hadoop cluster using Sahara. This option is available at the time of writing this book only for HDP and CDH clusters, which the chapter focuses on. It provides for each plugin a sample example by highlighting the requirements for each setup.

Chapter 7, Troubleshooting, provides best practices for troubleshooting Sahara when it generates errors during its setup and utilization. It starts by tackling major issues present in OpenStack that reflect many other components and how to escalate problem resolution using debugging tools and on-hand tips.

What you need for this book

This book assumes medium-level knowledge of Linux operating systems, basic knowledge of cloud computing and big data, and moderate experience with OpenStack software. The book will go through a simple multi-node setup of an OpenStack environment, which may require basic understanding of networking and virtualization concepts. If you have experience with Hadoop and Spark processes, it is a big plus. Although the book uses VirtualBox, feel free to use any other lab environment, such as VMware workstation or other tools.

OpenStack can be installed and runs either on bare metal or virtual machine. However, this book requires that you have enough resources for the whole setup. The minimum hardware or virtual requirements are listed as follows:

- CPU: 4 cores
- Memory: 8 GB of RAM
- Disk space: 80 GB

You will need the following software:

- Linux operating system: Centos 7.x.
- VirtualBox.
- The OpenStack RDO distribution, preferably the Liberty release. If you intend to use Juno or Kilo releases, make sure to change the plugin versions when launching clusters to comply within the right supported OpenStack version.

Internet connectivity is required to install the necessary OpenStack packages, Sahara images, and Sahara image packages for specific plugins.

Who this book is for

To use the content of this book, basic prior knowledge of OpenStack is expected. If you don't have that knowledge, it is always possible to catch up with the basic requirements by having a fast reading of the major components from the OpenStack community (`http://docs.openstack.org/admin-guide-cloud`). This covers the previous updates of OpenStack software, including the Juno, Kilo, and Liberty releases. This book is essentially intended for data scientists, big data architects, cloud developers, and DevOps engineers. If you are also willing to run your Hadoop and/or Spark clusters on top of OpenStack, then this book is ideal for you. If you already have a running OpenStack infrastructure, this book can help you quickly speed it up with Sahara.

Conventions

In this book, you will find a number of text styles that distinguish between different kinds of information. Here are some examples of these styles and an explanation of their meaning.

Code words in text, database table names, folder names, filenames, file extensions, pathnames, dummy URLs, user input, and Twitter handles are shown as follows: "Optionally, make sure to disable `NetworkManager` in your CentOS boxes."

A block of code is set as follows:

```
# nano worker_template_pp.json
{
 " name": "PP-Worker-Template",
  "flavor_id": "2",
  "plugin_name": "vanilla",
  "hadoop_version": "2.7.1",
  "node_processes": ["nodemanager", "datanode"],
  "auto_security_group": true
}
```

Any command-line input or output is written as follows:

```
# export IMAGE_ID=49fa54c0-18c0-4292-aa61-fa1a56dbfd24
# sahara image-register --id $IMAGE_ID --username centos
--description 'Sahara image CentOS 7 Hadoop Vanilla 2.7.1'
```

New terms and **important words** are shown in bold. Words that you see on the screen, for example, in menus or dialog boxes, appear in the text like this: "The first window in the wizard exposes the **Plugin name** and its version."

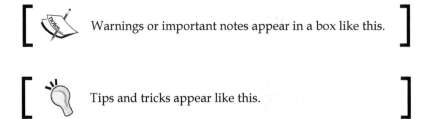

Warnings or important notes appear in a box like this.

Tips and tricks appear like this.

Reader feedback

Feedback from our readers is always welcome. Let us know what you think about this book—what you liked or disliked. Reader feedback is important for us as it helps us develop titles that you will really get the most out of.

To send us general feedback, simply e-mail feedback@packtpub.com, and mention the book's title in the subject of your message.

If there is a topic that you have expertise in and you are interested in either writing or contributing to a book, see our author guide at www.packtpub.com/authors.

Customer support

Now that you are the proud owner of a Packt book, we have a number of things to help you to get the most from your purchase.

Errata

Although we have taken every care to ensure the accuracy of our content, mistakes do happen. If you find a mistake in one of our books — maybe a mistake in the text or the code — we would be grateful if you could report this to us. By doing so, you can save other readers from frustration and help us improve subsequent versions of this book. If you find any errata, please report them by visiting http://www.packtpub.com/submit-errata, selecting your book, clicking on the **Errata Submission Form** link, and entering the details of your errata. Once your errata are verified, your submission will be accepted and the errata will be uploaded to our website or added to any list of existing errata under the Errata section of that title.

To view the previously submitted errata, go to https://www.packtpub.com/books/content/support and enter the name of the book in the search field. The required information will appear under the **Errata** section.

Piracy

Piracy of copyrighted material on the Internet is an ongoing problem across all media. At Packt, we take the protection of our copyright and licenses very seriously. If you come across any illegal copies of our works in any form on the Internet, please provide us with the location address or website name immediately so that we can pursue a remedy.

Please contact us at copyright@packtpub.com with a link to the suspected pirated material.

We appreciate your help in protecting our authors and our ability to bring you valuable content.

Questions

If you have a problem with any aspect of this book, you can contact us at questions@packtpub.com, and we will do our best to address the problem.

1
The Essence of Big Data in the Cloud

How to quantify data into business value? It's a serious question that we might be prompted to ask when we take a look around and notice the increasing appetite of users for rich media and the content of data across the web. That could generate several challenging points: How to manage the exponential amount of data? Particularly, how to extract from these immense waves of data the most valuable aspects? It is the era of big data! To meet the growing demand of big data and facilitate its analysis, few solutions such as Hadoop and Spark appeared and have become a necessary tool towards making a first successful step into the big data world. However, the first question was not sufficiently answered! It might be needed to introduce a new architecture and cost approach to respond to the scalability of intensive resources consumed when analyzing data. Although Hadoop, for example, is a great solution to run data analysis and processing, there are difficulties with configuration and maintenance. Besides, its complex architecture might require a lot of expertise. In this book, you will learn how to use OpenStack to manage and rapidly configure a Hadoop/Spark cluster. Sahara, the new OpenStack integrated project, offers an elegant self-service to deploy and manage big data clusters. It began as an Apache 2.0 project and now Sahara has joined the OpenStack ecosystem to provide a fast way of provisioning Hadoop clusters in the cloud. In this chapter, we will explore the following points:

- Introduce briefly the big data groove
- Understand the success of big data processing when it is combined with the cloud computing paradigm
- Learn how OpenStack can offer a unique big data management solution
- Discover Sahara in OpenStack and cover briefly the overall architecture

It is all about data

A world of information, sitting everywhere, in different formats and locations, generates a crucial question: where is my data?

During the last decade, most companies and organizations have started to realize the increasing rate of data generated every moment and have begun to switch to a more sophisticated way of handling the growing amount of information. Performing a given customer-business relationship in any organization depends strictly on answers found in their documents and files sitting on their hard drives. It is even wider, with data generating more data, where there comes the need to extract from it particular data elements. Therefore, the filtered elements will be stored separately for a better information management process, and will join the data space. We are talking about terabytes and petabytes of structured and unstructured data: that is the essence of big data.

The dimensions of big data

Big data refers to the data that overrides the scope of traditional data tools to manage and manipulate them.

Gartner analyst Doug Laney described big data in a research publication in 2001 in what is known as the 3Vs:

- **Volume**: The overall amount of data
- **Velocity**: The processing speed of data and the rate at which data arrives
- **Variety**: The different types of structured and unstructured data

To read more about the 3Vs concept introduced by Doug Laney, check the following link: http://blogs.gartner.com/doug-laney/files/2012/01/ad949-3D-Data-Management-Controlling-Data-Volume-Velocity-and-Variety.pdf

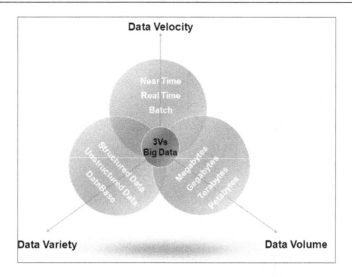

The big challenge of big data

Another important question is how will the data be manipulated and managed in a big space? For sure, traditional tools might need to be revisited to meet the large volume of data. In fact, loading and analyzing them in a traditional database means the database might become overwhelmed by the unstoppable massive surge of data.

Additionally, it is not only the volume of data that presents a challenge but also time and cost. Merging big data by using traditional tools might be too expensive, and the time taken to access data can be infinite. From a latency perspective, users need to run a query and get a response in a reasonable time. A different approach exists to meet those challenges: Hadoop.

The revolution of big data

Hadoop tools come to the rescue and answer a few challenging questions raised by big data. How can you store and manage a mixture of structured and unstructured data sitting across a vast storage network? How can given information be accessed quickly? How can you control the big data system in an enhanced scalable and flexible fashion?

The Hadoop framework lets data volumes increase while controlling the processing time. Without diving into the Hadoop technology stack, which is out of the scope of this book, it might be important to examine a few tools available under the umbrella of the Hadoop project and within its ecosystem:

- **Ambari**: Hadoop management and monitoring
- **Hadoop**: Hadoop distributed storage platform
- **HBase**: Hadoop NoSQL non-relational database
- **Hive**: Hadoop data warehouse
- **Hue**: Hadoop web interface for analyzing data
- **MapReduce**: Algorithm used by Hadoop MR component
- **Pig**: Data analysis high-level language
- **Storm**: Distributed real-time computation system
- **Yarn**: MapReduce in Hadoop version 2
- **ZooKeeper**: Hadoop centralized configuration system
- **Flume**: Service mechanism for data collection and streaming
- **Mahout**: Scalable machine learning platform
- **Avro**: Data serialization platform

Apache Spark is another amazing alternative to process large amounts of data that a typical MapReduce cannot provide. Typically, Spark can run on top of Hadoop or standalone. Hadoop uses HDFS as its default file system. It is designed as a distributed file system that provides a high throughput access to application data.

The big data tools (Hadoop/Spark) sound very promising. On the other hand, while launching a project on a terabyte-scale, it might go quickly into a petabyte-scale. A traditional solution is found by adding more clusters. However, operational teams may face more difficulties with manual deployment, change management and most importantly, performance scaling. Ideally, when actively working on a live production setup, users should not experience any sort of service disruption. Adding then an *elasticity* flavor to the Hadoop infrastructure in a scalable way is imperative. How can you achieve this? An innovative idea is using the cloud.

Some of the most recent functional programming languages are Scala and R. Scala can be used to develop applications that interact with Hadoop and Spark. R language has become very popular for data analysis, data processing, and descriptive statistics. Integration of Hadoop with R is ongoing; **RHadoop** is one of the R open source projects that exposes a rich collection of packages to help the analysis of data with Hadoop. To read more about RHadoop, visit the official GitHub project page found at `https://github.com/RevolutionAnalytics/RHadoop/wiki`

A key of big data success

Cloud computing technology might be a satisfactory solution by eliminating large upfront IT investments. A scalable approach is essential to let businesses easily scale out infrastructure. This can be simple by putting the application in the cloud and letting the provider supports and resolves the big data management scalability problem.

Use case: Elastic MapReduce

One shining example is the popular Amazon service named **Elastic MapReduce** (**EMR**), which can be found at `https://aws.amazon.com/elasticmapreduce/`. Amazon EMR in a nutshell is Hadoop in the cloud. Before taking a step further and seeing briefly how such technology works, it might be essential to check where EMR sits in Amazon from an architectural level.

Basically, Amazon offers the famous EC2 service (which stands for Elastic Compute Cloud) that can be found at `https://aws.amazon.com/ec2/`. It's a way that you can demand a certain size of computations resources, servers, load balancers, and many more. Moreover, Amazon exposes a simple key/value storage model named **Simple Storage Service (S3)** that can be found at `https://aws.amazon.com/s3/`.

Using S3, storing any type of data is very simple and straightforward using web or command-line interfaces. It is the responsibility of Amazon to take care of the scaling, data availability, and the reliability of the storage service.

We have used a few acronyms: EC2, S3 and EMR. From high-level architecture, **EMR** sits on top of **EC2** and **S3**. It uses EC2 for processing and S3 for storage. The main purpose of EMR is to process data in the cloud without managing your own infrastructure. As described briefly in the following diagram, data is being pulled from S3 and is going to automatically spin up an EC2 cluster within a certain size. The results will be piped back to S3. The hallmark of Hadoop in the cloud is zero touch infrastructure. What you need to do is just specify what kind of job you intend to run, the location of the data, and from where to pick up the results.

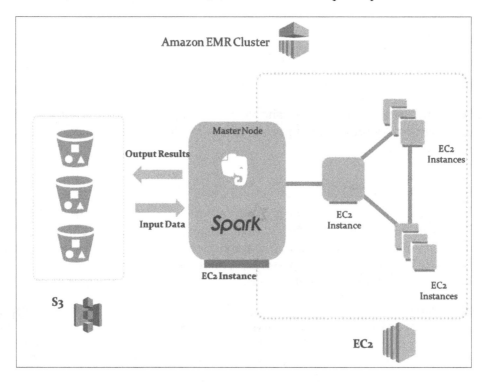

OpenStack crossing big data

OpenStack is a very promising open source cloud computing solution that does not stop adumbrating and joining different projects related to the cloud environment. OpenStack kept growing its ecosystem thanks to the conglomeration of many projects that make it a very rich cloud platform. OpenStack exposes several infrastructure management services that work in tandem to provide a complete suite of infrastructure management software. Most of its modules have been refined and become more mature within the Havana release. It might be essential first to itemize the most basic ones briefly:

- **Keystone**: The identity management service. Connecting and using OpenStack services requires in the first place authentication.

- **Glance**: The image management service. Instances will be launched from disk images that glance stores them in its image catalogue.

- **Nova**: The instance management service. Once authenticated, a user can create an instance by defining basic resources such as image and network.

- **Cinder**: The block storage management service. It allows creating and attaching volumes to instances. It also handles snapshots, which can be used as a boot source.

- **Neutron**: The network management service. It allows creating and managing an isolated virtual network for each tenant in an OpenStack deployment.

- **Swift**: The object storage management service. Any form of data in Swift is stored in a redundant, scalable, distributed object storage using a cluster of servers.

- **Heat**: The orchestration service. It provides a fast-paced way to launch a complete stack from one single template file.

- **Ceilometer**: The telemetry service. It monitors the cluster resources used in an OpenStack deployment.

- **Horizon**: The OpenStack Dashboard. It provides a web-based interface to different OpenStack services such as Keystone, Glance, Nova, Cinder, Neutron, Swift, Heat, and so on.

- **Trove**: The **Database as a Service (DBaaS)** component in OpenStack. It enables users to consume relational and non-relational database engines on top of OpenStack.

> At the time of writing, more incubated projects are being integrated in the OpenStack ecosystem with the Liberty release such as Ironic, Zaqar, Manilla, Designate, Barbican, Murano, Magnum, Kolla, and Congress. To read more about those projects, refer to the official OpenStack website at:
> `https://www.openstack.org/software/project-navigator/`

The awesomeness of OpenStack comes not only from its modular architecture but also the contribution of its large community by developing and integrating a new project in nearly every new OpenStack release. Within the Icehouse release, OpenStack contributors turned on the light to meet the big data world: the Elastic Data Processing service. That becomes even more amazing to see a cloud service similar to EMR in Amazon running by OpenStack.

Well, it is time to open the curtains and explore the marriage of one of the most popular big data programs, Hadoop, with one of the most successful cloud operating system OpenStack: Sahara. As shown in the next diagram of the OpenStack **IaaS** (short for **Infrastructure as a Service**) layering schema, Sahara can be expressed as an optional service that sits on top of the base components of OpenStack. It can be enabled or activated when running a private cloud based on OpenStack.

> More details on Sahara integration in a running OpenStack environment will be discussed in *Chapter 2, Integrating OpenStack Sahara.*

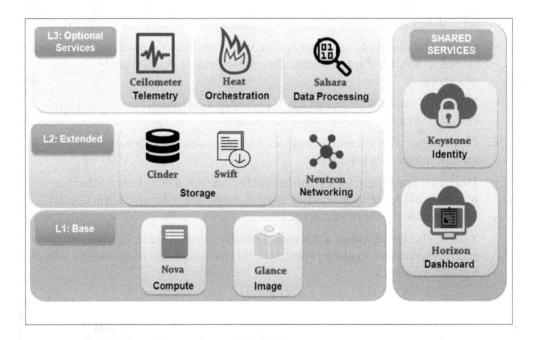

Sahara: bringing big data to the cloud

Sahara is an incubated project for big data processing since the OpenStack Icehouse release. It has been integrated since the OpenStack Juno release. The Sahara project was a joint effort and contribution between Mirantis, a major OpenStack integration company, Red Hat, and Hortonworks. The Sahara project enables users to run Hadoop/Spark big data applications on top of OpenStack.

The Sahara project was named **Savanna** and has been renamed due to trademark issues.

Sahara in OpenStack

The main reason the Sahara project was born is the need for agile access to big data. By moving big data to the cloud, we can capture many benefits for the user experience in this case:

- **Unlimited scalability**: Sahara sits on top of the OpenStack Cloud management platform. By its nature, OpenStack services scale very well. As we will see, Sahara lets Hadoop clusters scale on OpenStack.

- **Elasticity**: Growing or shrinking, as required, a Hadoop cluster is obviously a major advantage of using Sahara.

- **Data availability**: Sahara is tightly integrated with core OpenStack services as we will see later. Swift presents a real cloud storage solution and can be used by Hadoop clusters for data source storage. It is a highly durable and available option when considering the input/output of processing a data workflow.

 Swift can be used for input and output data source access in a Hadoop cluster for all job types except Hive.

For an intimate understanding of the benefits cited previously, it might be essential to go through a concise architectural overview of Sahara in OpenStack. As depicted in the next diagram, a user can access and manage big data resources from the Horizon web UI or the OpenStack command-line interface. To use any service in OpenStack, it is required to authenticate against the Keystone service. It also applies to Sahara, which it needs to be registered with the Keystone service catalogue.

To be able to create a Hadoop cluster, Sahara will need to retrieve and register virtual machine images in its own image registry by contacting Glance. Nova is also another essential OpenStack core component to provision and launch virtual machines for the Hadoop cluster. Additionally, Heat can be used by Sahara in order to automate the deployment of a Hadoop cluster, which will be covered in a later chapter.

 In OpenStack within the Juno release, it is possible to instruct Sahara to use block storage as nodes backend.

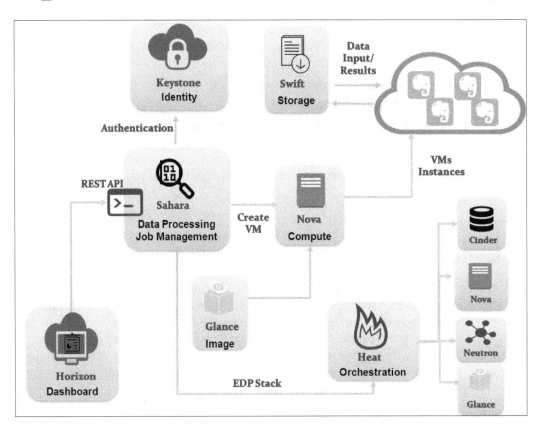

The Sahara OpenStack mission

In addition to sharing the aforementioned generic big data in OpenStack, OpenStack Sahara has some unique characteristics that can be itemized as the following:

- **Fast provisioning**: Deploying a Hadoop/Spark cluster becomes an easy task by performing a few push-button clicks or via command line interface.

- **Centralized management**: Controlling and monitoring a Hadoop/Spark cluster from one single management interface efficiently.

- **Cluster management**: Sahara offers an amazing *templating* mechanism. Starting, stopping, scaling, shaping, and resizing actions may form the life cycle of a Hadoop/Spark cluster ecosystem. Performing such a life cycle in a repeatable way can be simplified by using a template in which will be defined the Hadoop configuration. All the proper cluster node setup details just get out of the way of the user.

- **Workload management**: This is another key feature of Sahara. It basically defines the Elastic Data Processing, the running and queuing jobs, and how they should work in the cluster. Several types of jobs for data processing such as MapReduce job, Pig script, Oozie, JAR file, and many others should run across a defined cluster. Sahara enables the provisioning of a new ephemeral cluster and terminates it on demand, for example, running the job for some specific analysis and shutting down the cluster when the job is finished. Workload management encloses data sources that defines where the job is going to read data from and write them to.

 Data sources URLs into Swift and URLs into HDFS will be discovered in more details in *Chapter 5, Discovering Advanced Features with Sahara*.

- **No deep expertise**: Administrators and operators will not wonder anymore about managing the infrastructure running underneath the Hadoop/Spark cluster. With Sahara, managing the infrastructure does not require real big data operational expertise.

- **Multi-framework support**: Sahara exposes the possibility to integrate diverse data processing frameworks using provisioning plugins. A user can choose to deploy a specific Hadoop/Spark distribution such as the **Hortonworks Data Platform (HDP)** plugin via Ambari, Spark, Vanilla, MapR Distribution, and Cloudera plugins.

- **Analytics as a Service**: Bursty analytics workloads can utilize free computing infrastructure capacity for a limited period of time.

The Sahara's architecture

We have seen in the previous diagram how Sahara has been integrated in the OpenStack ecosystem from a high-level perspective. As it is a new OpenStack service, Sahara exposes different components that interact as the client of other OpenStack services such as **Keystone**, **Swift**, **Nova**, **Neutron**, **Glance**, and **Cinder**. Every request initiated from the Sahara endpoint is performed on the OpenStack services public APIs. For this reason, it is essential to put under scope the Sahara architecture as shown in the following diagram:

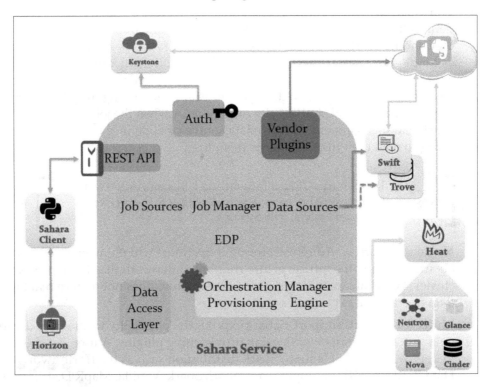

The OpenStack Sahara architecture consists essentially of the following components:

- **REST API**: Every client request initiated from the dashboard will be translated to a **REST API** call.

- **Auth**: Like any other OpenStack service, Sahara must authenticate against the authentication service **Keystone**. This also includes client and user authorization to use the Sahara service.

- **Vendor Plugins**: The vendor plugins sit in the middle of the Sahara architecture that exposes the type of cluster to be launched. Vendors such as Cloudera and Apache Ambari provide their distributions in Sahara so users can configure and launch a Hadoop based on their plugin mechanism.

- **Elastic Data Processing (EDP)**: Enables the running of jobs on an existing and launched Hadoop or Spark cluster in Sahara. EDP makes sure that jobs are scheduled to the clusters and maintain the status of jobs, their sources, from where the data sources should be extracted, and to where the output of the treated data sources should be written.

- **Orchestration Manager/Provisioning Engine**: The core component of the Sahara cluster provisioning and management. It instructs the **Heat** engine (OpenStack orchestrator service) to provision a cluster by communicating with the rest of the OpenStack services including compute, network, block storage, and images services.

- **Data Access Layer (DAL)**: Persistent internal Sahara data store.

 It is important to note that Sahara was configured to use a direct engine to create instances of the cluster which initiate calls to the required OpenStack services to provision the instances. It is also important to note that Direct Engine in Sahara will be deprecated from OpenStack Liberty release where Heat becomes the default Sahara provisioning engine.

Summary

In this chapter, you explored the factors behind the success of the emerging technology of data processing and analysis using cloud computing technology. You learned how OpenStack can be a great opportunity to offer the needed scalable and elastic big data on-demand infrastructure. It can be also useful to execute on-demand Elastic Data Processing tasks.

The first chapter exposed the new OpenStack incubated project called Sahara: a rapid, auto-deploy, and scalable solution for Hadoop and Spark clusters. An overall view of the Sahara architecture has been discussed for a fast-paced understanding of the platform and how it works in an OpenStack private cloud environment.

Now it is time to get things running and discover how such an amazing big data management solution can be used by installing OpenStack and integrating Sahara, which will be the topic of the next chapter.

2
Integrating OpenStack Sahara

So far, we discovered in the first chapter what makes sense of the big data groove in the cloud and more specifically in OpenStack. The *Elastic Hadoop on demand* service called **Sahara** was introduced and we covered how it was architecturally integrated in OpenStack. In this chapter, we will walk through a complete setup and configuration of Sahara in OpenStack. To do so, a complete OpenStack environment setup is required in the first place before integrating Sahara.

Installing OpenStack and configuring it manually is a repetitive and sometimes an error-prone process, especially within the last releases that include more incubated projects and running more services. Getting the OpenStack environment up and running can take a few dozen pages and a lot of troubleshooting issues. On the other hand, being a proponent of the automation discipline and tools is a good step in the right direction for a fast, consistent, and correct installation process. There are several ways to automate the installation and configuration of OpenStack using different system management tools and distributions thanks to the contribution of many open source communities and third parties. The installation process can be achieved automatically using some of DevOps' installers such as Chef, Puppet, Juju, and SaltStack. For OpenStack development purposes, DevStack and ANVIL are fast alternatives to provide a complete core development environment for developers. Fuel is also a good automated option to deploy and get a large-scale OpenStack environment up and running. Some other distributions are commercial products that provide a complete, stable, and ready for production OpenStack environment such as Red Hat Enterprise Linux OpenStack Platform, Cisco OpenStack Private Cloud, HP Helion OpenStack, and many more.

You can use the solution that you feel most comfortable with if you have already installed or used OpenStack. On the other hand, we will use in this chapter a community-supported distribution of OpenStack called RDO. It is simply a Red Hat and Fedora derived from (such as CentOS distributions) analogue to Enterprise Linux to build OpenStack on Red Hat. The RDO project is an open source and community-supported distribution of OpenStack that packages its code in each of the upstream releases of OpenStack. This chapter will cover the following:

- Preparing the test infrastructure environment
- Installing OpenStack environment using RDO
- Installing Sahara and integrating it in OpenStack

Preparing the test infrastructure environment

Before going directly to the installation process, it might be necessary to check how the OpenStack environment will be deployed. This is very important to plan in advance in order to get our private cloud lab consistent without any errors. OpenStack is very modular and can be deployed in many ways.

Depending on your needs and requirements, the installation can be diversified in different layouts and topologies. For example, networking in OpenStack is becoming very advanced and a lack of understanding of one of the major components and plugins might lead to non-functional infrastructure especially when it comes to launch instances. Covering the different architectures of OpenStack is out of the scope of this book. The OpenStack portal www.openstack.org exposes very rich and detailed content on different designs approaches. However, it is essential to start with a minimal architecture in a basic environment for test purposes. Therefore, it is possible to expand it and scale it out.

OpenStack test topology environment

The installation of the OpenStack environment involves the combination of different nodes as follows:

- **Cloud controller**: Runs most of the OpenStack services such as identity, image, and orchestration services. It can also run the queuing and databases services. Optionally, it supports other management portions of networking, storage, monitoring, and compute services.

- **Compute node**: The compute node runs the hypervisor where the instances will run. The compute node can also run a network agent in order to connect instances to their associated tenant networks. Compute node can be multiple for higher computation capacity.

- **Network node**: In case of using Neutron in a production environment, it might be required to set up a separate network node that provides switching and routing capabilities. The network node use case is very useful when you plan to extend the physical network and build an environment with multiple levels of networking services.

- **Storage nodes**: Object storage (Swift) or block storage (Cinder) can be separately deployed in dedicated storage clusters. The controller nodes can run storage service as well. However, in a large and highly scalable environment, it might be necessary to leave the storage mission out of the cloud controller box. This is an extended layout and depends on the purpose of the cloud itself.

For the sake of simplicity, we will go through a simple setup using only two nodes: a cloud controller node that will hold both network and storage services and a first compute node. However, running all the OpenStack services in one box might not be recommended. We should think about deploying a Hadoop cluster later, which might require an extra dedicated compute power and network performance. In addition, we will need a separate compute node to scale up and down seamlessly without bothering the cloud controller resources and risk performance degradation. Although it will be a test environment, mimicking a production one is always useful to understand how such a system should work and avoid surprises in the future.

OpenStack test networking layout

Planning the overall test networking setup for our test environment will define how many network interfaces should exist in each node. At least four network traffic types should exist in an OpenStack infrastructure, as follows:

- **Public network**: An external network that allows instances to reach the Internet.

- **Management network**: It allows inter-communication between hosts running OpenStack services. In our case, compute node needs to reach the messaging and database service, which requires communicating through this network.

- **VM network**: Also called Guest network. This is a very dedicated network for instances traffic. Traffic restriction using VLAN tagged networks or the implementation of the virtual overlay networks (VXLAN and GRE) encapsulation can go through the VM network.

- **API network**: OpenStack relies essentially on APIs. All the OpenStack services are exposed either to users or services via endpoints through the API network.

Optionally, a dedicated network for storage can also be added to the preceding list when it is necessary to implement separate large-scale storage clusters in the OpenStack cloud environment. For the sake of simplicity, we will set up the OpenStack environment using three different interfaces per host:

- **eth0**: Will serve the Public and VM networks

- **eth1**: Will serve the Management and API networks

- **eth2**: Will serve the External network for the cloud controller and the compute nodes to download packages

Note: Using a single interface per node will result in bad performance and system degradation. Although it can be useful for a fast proof of concept in a test environment, the risk failure is still high. If you intend to run in a mono-interface mode, be sure to check first the total bandwidth and monitor its consumption when launching instances. It is also possible to combine all the OpenStack networks in one NIC and keep the external network in a different virtual NIC interface.

OpenStack test environment design

So far, we have decided on our overall topology and the network layout. Now, let's summarize our design in the following diagram:

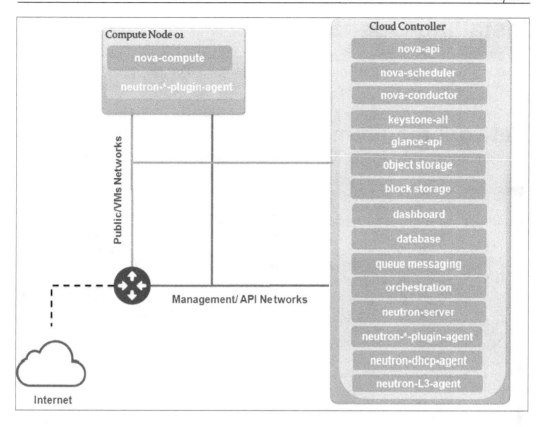

The previous diagram illustrates a minimal version design for the OpenStack environment. It is important to notice that the **Cloud Controller** also held network services through Neutron. You might be tempted to think that nova-network can be used as well; however, preparing to handle a big data environment in a cloud environment using Sahara might require better networking management and capabilities such as switching and routing, which are offered by Neutron. Both **Cloud Controller** and **Compute Node** use two different interfaces and can be connected to an external router to handle routing between the network segments.

To learn more about the Neutron networking component in OpenStack, refer to this link: `http://docs.openstack.org/liberty/networking-guide/intro-os-networking.html`

Installing OpenStack

For our test environment setup, we will use VirtualBox. So, we will run both the cloud controller and compute node in virtual machines. For a proper and stable setup, it might be necessary to go through a few system requirements first.

Network requirements

Since we are using VirtualBox, the physical host must have access to the Internet.

Since CentOS/RHEL 6, a predictable network device naming rule has been introduced for network interfaces. It is adopted by default on CentOS/RHEL 7. For the sake of simplicity, it would be more practical to control the naming conventions of network interfaces by assigning simple and easy names. In order to rename an interface on CentOS/RHEL 7, disable the predictable naming rule by editing the /etc/default/grub file and passing the net.ifnames=0 kernel parameter to the GRUB_CMDLINE_LINUX variable when the system boots. Regenerate the GRUB configuration with the updated kernel parameters using the grub2-mkconfig command-line tool. Add a new line per each device name in the /etc/udev/rules.d/70-persistent-net.rules file within its MAC address. For example, changing a network interface named eno16777984 on CentOS 7 to eth0 can be done on the /etc/udev/rules.d/70-persistent-net.rules file by adding the following line:

```
SUBSYSTEM=="net", ACTION=="add", DRIVERS=="?*", AT
TR{address}=="00:50:56:a6:72:c3", ATTR{type}=="1",
KERNEL=="eth*", NAME="eth0"
```

The networks in the VirtualBox environment can be a bit confusing. In order to mimic exactly a real-world deployment as was designed previously, it might be necessary to take a look at the following diagram:

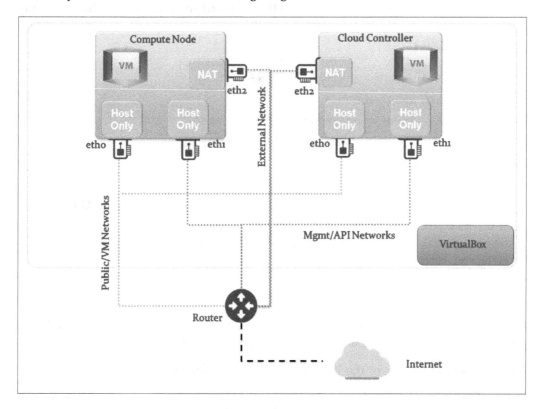

The VirtualBox offers different network settings. The **eth0** network interface will be **Host Only**. The network segment will carry **VM** data and allows it to connect to the external network. Additionally, in order to allow VMs to communicate internally, it is required to set **Promiscuous mode** for **eth0** and **eth1** to **Allow All** as the following:

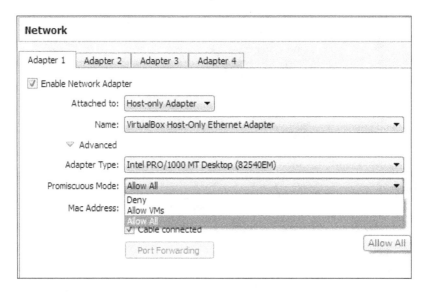

eth1 can be configured as Host-only as well. eth2 will allow an external connection for both virtual machines to download packages from the Internet.

The next table summarizes the IP addressing schema for each host interface:

Hostname	Interface	Adapter type	IP Address
Cloud controller	eth0	Host-only	10.10.10.47/24
Cloud controller	eth1	Host-only	10.20.10.47/24
Cloud controller	eth2	NAT	DHCP
Compute node	eth0	Host-only	10.10.10.48/24
Compute node	eth1	Host-only	10.20.10.48/24
Compute node	eth2	NAT	DHCP

 VirtualBox runs internally a DHCP server to assign IP addresses to the virtual machine. In NAT mode, the eth2 interface will be connected to a private network, by default 10.0.X.0/24, where X corresponds to the instance of the NAT interface.

System requirements

Running OpenStack on virtual machines can be a fast solution for a proof of concept. However, it might be needed to check the capabilities of the host machine itself in the first place in order to assign minimal resources for each cloud controller and compute node. Depending on the host hardware specifications, the following requirements should be met:

- Cloud controller:
  - Processor: 64-bit x86
  - Memory: 3 GB RAM
  - Disk space: 40 GB
  - Network: Three virtual NICS

- Compute node:
  - Processor: 64-bit x86
  - Memory: 4 GB RAM
  - Disk space: 40 GB
  - Network: Three virtual NICS

The current setup will use QEMU for nova hypervisor in OpenStack. If you intend to use KVM, make sure to extend virtualization feature on the physical CPU to VirtualBox virtual CPU as nested virtualization. Be sure to **Enable VT-x/AMD-v** virtualization technologies on VirtualBox for both nodes. Doing this will update the BIOS of the nodes to support virtualization capability.

> Check each host CPU is equipped with the hardware virtualization extensions that are required for the KVM hypervisor in compute node. It is possible to run the following command line on the compute node:
>
> `# egrep '(vmx|svm)' --color /proc/cpuinfo`
>
> It required to see on from the output either vmx or svm flag.

This can be found as shown in the following screen:

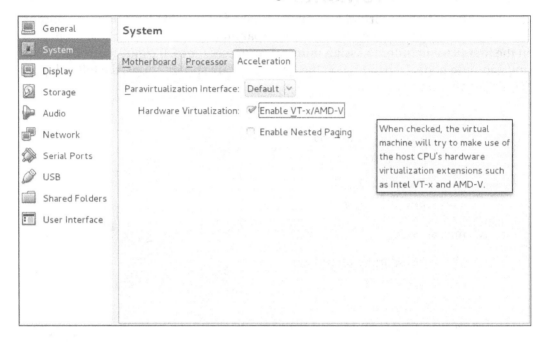

CentOS 7 operating system minimal installation will be used, which can be found at https://www.centos.org/download/. The kernel version used is 2.6.32-431.11.2.el6.x86_64.

Once CentOS 7 is installed on each VM, update the yum repository and reboot both nodes. Make sure to assign hostnames for each node by editing the /etc/hostname file and adding host FQDN entries to the /etc/hosts file in each machine. For example, the cloud controller virtual machine has the following /etc/hosts content:

```
10.10.10.47 cc.pp
10.10.10.48 cn.pp
```

We intend to install and use the Liberty OpenStack release.

 Before using the RDO script installation tool, check the ssh connectivity between both virtual machines through the eth0 network interface.

Running the RDO installation

RDO exposes an amazing install OpenStack tool called Packstack. Briefly, it connects to each node on its discovery list via SSH and runs puppet to install and configure OpenStack. The following step-by-step walkthrough will guide you to help bring OpenStack up and running:

1. Before running the Packstack command line, we will need to update and install the latest stable RDO release rpm on the cloud controller node as follows:

    ```
    # sudo yum install -y https://rdoproject.org/repos/rdo-release.rpm
    ```

    ```
    #sudo yum update -y
    ```

    ```
    #sudo rpm -ivh  https://repos.fedorapeople.org/repos/openstack/
    openstack-liberty/rdo-release-liberty-1.noarch.rpm
    ```

2. Next, we will install the Packstack tools as follows:

    ```
    # sudo yum install -y openstack-packstack
    ```

3. Instead of running Packstack directly, we are going to perform a few extra configuration steps. Basically, Packstack will use a sample suite of configuration directives detailed in an answer file. To generate a new answer file, run the following command line:

    ```
    # packstack --gen-answer-file answers_pp.txt
    ```

4. At this stage, we have a generated Packstack answer file that we will need to edit. Remember, we are aiming to add a new compute node and use Neutron for the networking service in OpenStack.

    To use the Neutron networking overlay and VXLAN tunneling, edit the answers_pp.txt file as the following:

    ```
    CONFIG_NEUTRON_SERVER_HOST=10.10.10.47
    CONFIG_NEUTRON_L3_HOSTS=10.10.10.47
    CONFIG_NEUTRON_METADATA_HOSTS=10.10.10.47
    CONFIG_NEUTRON_OVS_TENANT_NETWORK_TYPE=vxlan
    CONFIG_NEUTRON_OVS_TUNNEL_RANGES=1:1000
    CONFIG_NEUTRON_OVS_TUNNEL_IF=eth0
    ```

    To use the openvswitch plugin, edit the following directive:

    ```
    CONFIG_NEUTRON_L2_PLUGIN=openvswitch
    ```

    To reflect the test environment architecture, edit the answers_pp.txt file as the following:

    ```
    CONFIG_NOVA_COMPUTE_HOSTS=10.10.10.48
    ```

Before running the packstack install, we will need to enable other components that will be used in later chapters like Heat and Swift as the following:

```
CONFIG_SWIFT_INSTALL=y
CONFIG_HEAT_INSTALL=y
```

5. Optionally, make sure to disable `NetworkManager` in your CentOS boxes:

```
# systemctl disable NetworkManager.service
```

6. Additionally, SELinux might raise a few communication problems among services in the OpenStack multi-node environment. Thus, at least changing SELinux to permissive mode on both boxes will save a lot of troubleshooting time later on.

To do so, run the following command line in both the cloud controller and compute nodes:

```
# sed -i "s/SELINUX=enforcing/c\SELINUX=permissive" /etc/selinux/
config
```

It is not advised to disable completely SELinux on production servers. However, for fast testing purposes, SELinux can be disabled and the adjusted policies applied.

SELinux can take one of the three following states:

- **Enforcing**: Security policy is loaded and enforced.
- **Permissive**: Security policy is loaded but not enforced. The mode generates warning logs. It is mostly used for testing and debugging purposes.
- **Disabled**: Security policy is not loaded. The system is vulnerable to security threats.

7. Save the file and run the packstack by invoking the `answer_pp.txt` file as follows:

```
# packstack --answer-file answer_pp.txt
```

Find a quick start to install the OpenStack all-in-one box here: https://www.rdoproject.org/Quickstart

```
Welcome to the Packstack setup utility

The installation log file is available at: /var/tmp/packstack/20150929-142929-19V9oc/opens

Installing:
Clean Up                                                [ DONE ]
Discovering ip protocol version                         [ DONE ]
Setting up ssh keys                                     [ DONE ]
Preparing servers                                       [ DONE ]
Pre installing Puppet and discovering hosts' details    [ DONE ]
Adding pre install manifest entries                     [ DONE ]
Setting up CACERT                                       [ DONE ]
Adding AMQP manifest entries                            [ DONE ]
Adding MariaDB manifest entries                         [ DONE ]
Fixing Keystone LDAP config parameters to be undef if empty[ DONE ]
Adding Keystone manifest entries                        [ DONE ]
Adding Glance Keystone manifest entries                 [ DONE ]
Adding Glance manifest entries                          [ DONE ]
Adding Cinder Keystone manifest entries                 [ DONE ]
Checking if the Cinder server has a cinder-volumes vg[ DONE ]
Adding Cinder manifest entries                          [ DONE ]
Adding Nova API manifest entries                        [ DONE ]
Adding Nova Keystone manifest entries                   [ DONE ]
Adding Nova Cert manifest entries                       [ DONE ]
Adding Nova Conductor manifest entries                  [ DONE ]
Creating ssh keys for Nova migration                    [ DONE ]
Gathering ssh host keys for Nova migration              [ DONE ]
Adding Nova Compute manifest entries                    [ DONE ]
Adding Nova Scheduler manifest entries                  [ DONE ]
Adding Nova VNC Proxy manifest entries                  [ DONE ]
Adding OpenStack Network-related Nova manifest entries[ DONE ]
Adding Nova Common manifest entries                     [ DONE ]
Adding Neutron FWaaS Agent manifest entries             [ DONE ]
Adding Neutron LBaaS Agent manifest entries             [ DONE ]
Adding Neutron API manifest entries                     [ DONE ]
Adding Neutron Keystone manifest entries                [ DONE ]
Adding Neutron L3 manifest entries                      [ DONE ]
Adding Neutron L2 Agent manifest entries                [ DONE ]
Adding Neutron DHCP Agent manifest entries              [ DONE ]
Adding Neutron Metering Agent manifest entries          [ DONE ]
Adding Neutron Metadata Agent manifest entries          [ DONE ]
Checking if NetworkManager is enabled and running       [ DONE ]
Adding OpenStack Client manifest entries                [ DONE ]
Adding Horizon manifest entries                         [ DONE ]
```

Once Packstack is executed, it ensures connectivity to the nodes described in the answer file. In our case: the cloud controller and compute node. Therefore, it passes to generate manifest entries. The hallmark of such a command tool is the ability to roll back when a failure event occurs during installation. It is still always possible to adjust or correct a certain number of parameters in the answer file and rerun Packstack.

Remember that Packstack runs puppet to deploy the OpenStack nodes. Thus, the previous figure illustrates several lines showing the preparation of the required manifest files that will invoke puppet to run and configure the nodes based on the configuration definitions.

The Packstack installation process might take some time; if everything goes well, we can see at the end the following output:

```
Applying 192.168.120.253_postscript.pp
Applying 192.168.120.254_postscript.pp
192.168.120.253_postscript.pp:                      [ DONE ]
192.168.120.254_postscript.pp:                      [ DONE ]
Applying Puppet manifests                           [ DONE ]
Finalizing                                          [ DONE ]

 **** Installation completed successfully ******
```

Additionally, run the openstack-status command-line tool to check the status of every OpenStack service. First, populate the environment variables included in the generated keystone admin file as follows:

```
# source keystonerc_admin

# openstack-status

== Nova services ==

openstack-nova-api:               active

openstack-nova-cert:              active

openstack-nova-compute:           active

openstack-nova-network:           inactive   (disabled on boot)

openstack-nova-scheduler:         active

openstack-nova-conductor:         active

== Glance services ==

openstack-glance-api:             active

openstack-glance-registry:        active

== Keystone service ==

openstack-keystone:               active

== Horizon service ==

openstack-dashboard:              active

== neutron services ==

neutron-server:                   active

neutron-dhcp-agent:               active
```

```
neutron-13-agent:                        active
neutron-metadata-agent:                  active
neutron-openvswitch-agent:               active
== Swift services ==
openstack-swift-proxy:                   active
openstack-swift-account:                 active
openstack-swift-container:               active
openstack-swift-object:                  active
== Cinder services ==
openstack-cinder-api:                    active
openstack-cinder-scheduler:              active
openstack-cinder-volume:                 active
openstack-cinder-backup:                 active
```

Here we go. We can check easily from the previous Packstack command-line output a successful installation of OpenStack deployed in two nodes: the cloud controller and compute node. On the other hand, it might be interesting to verify the correctness of the compute node installation.

In a new terminal, ssh to the compute node and run the following command line:

```
# tail -f /var/log/nova/nova-compute.log
```

```
- -] Compute_service record updated for ('oss.data', 'oss.data')
- -] Compute service record updated for oss.data:oss.data
- - - - -] Connecting to AMQP server on 10.10.10.47:5672
- - - - -] Connected to AMQP server on 10.10.10.47:5672
```

We can see clearly that the nova-compute service is able to join the messaging queue service AMQP running on the cloud controller.

When the Packstack installer finalizes a successful installation of the OpenStack environment, a new file is created on the controller node named keystonerc_admin.

This file contains the administrative user's credentials to enable access to the OpenStack dashboard. An exemplar of the credentials file can be shown as the following using the `cat` command line:

```
# cat keystonerc_admin
unset OS_SERVICE_TOKEN
export OS_USERNAME=admin
export OS_PASSWORD=19868b7617434823
export OS_AUTH_URL=http://10.10.10.47:5000/v2.0
export PS1='[\u@\h \W(keystone_admin)]\$ '
```

Using a web browser, point to the IP address configured and shown previously to access the OpenStack dashboard:

By entering the mentioned username/password exposed in the credentials file, it will be possible to access the OpenStack dashboard and start to manage your test private cloud environment:

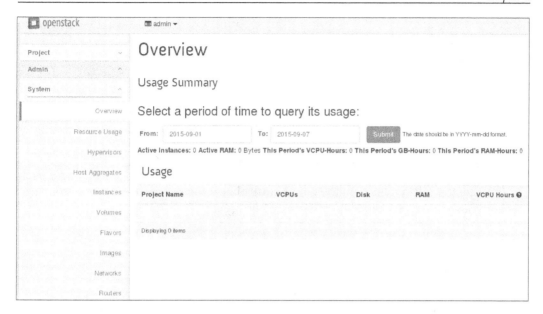

Integrating Sahara

In this section, the Sahara service will be installed and configured in the cloud controller node. To do so, a few steps need to be done in order to get a successful Sahara service integration in our OpenStack environment.

Installing and configuring OpenStack Sahara

The RDO installation did not provide any *Elastic Data Processing* installation. Thus, we will need to install the right OpenStack Sahara package from the repository in the cloud controller node as follows:

```
# yum install openstack-sahara
```

The openstack-sahara package provides essentially the openstack-sahara-api to talk with other OpenStack services as well as the **Command Line Interface (CLI)** clients sahara and sahara-db-manage.

The next step requires proper configuration to connect to the database. Like any other OpenStack service, the database connection URI directive can be found in the service configuration file, which in our case is in /etc/sahara/sahara.conf.

1. Since we are using MySQL, add the following line to /etc/sahara/sahara.conf:

   # DATABASE

   [database]

   connection=mysql://sahara:sahara@10.10.10.47/sahara

2. Use the mysql client on the cloud controller node to create a Sahara database:

   MariaDB [(none)]> CREATE DATABASE sahara;

   MariaDB [(none)]> GRANT ALL ON sahara.* TO 'sahara'@'%' IDENTIFIED BY 'sahara';

   MariaDB [(none)]> flush privileges;

3. At this stage, it might be necessary to create the database schema as the following:

   # sahara-db-manage –config-file /etc/sahara/sahara.conf upgrade head

   The following output might help to trace the database connection URI process:

```
INFO [alembic.migration] Context impl MySQLImpl.
INFO [alembic.migration] Will assume non-transactional DDL.
INFO [alembic.migration] Running upgrade  -> 001, Icehouse release
INFO [alembic.migration] Running upgrade 001 -> 002, placeholder
INFO [alembic.migration] Running upgrade 002 -> 003, placeholder
INFO [alembic.migration] Running upgrade 003 -> 004, placeholder
INFO [alembic.migration] Running upgrade 004 -> 005, placeholder
INFO [alembic.migration] Running upgrade 005 -> 006, placeholder
INFO [alembic.migration] Running upgrade 006 -> 007, convert clusters.status_description to LongText
INFO [alembic.migration] Running upgrade 007 -> 008, add security_groups field to node groups
INFO [alembic.migration] Running upgrade 008 -> 009, add rollback info to cluster
INFO [alembic.migration] Running upgrade 009 -> 010, add auto_security_groups flag to node group
INFO [alembic.migration] Running upgrade 010 -> 011, add Sahara settings info to cluster
INFO [alembic.migration] Running upgrade 011 -> 012, add availability_zone field to node groups
INFO [alembic.migration] Running upgrade 012 -> 013, add volumes_availability_zone field to node groups
INFO [alembic.migration] Running upgrade 013 -> 014, add_volume_type
INFO [alembic.migration] Running upgrade 014 -> 015, add_events_objects
INFO [alembic.migration] Running upgrade 015 -> 016, Add is_proxy_gateway
INFO [alembic.migration] Running upgrade 016 -> 017, drop progress in JobExecution
INFO [alembic.migration] Running upgrade 017 -> 018, add volume_local_to_instance flag
INFO [alembic.migration] Running upgrade 018 -> 019, Add is_default field for cluster and node_group templates
INFO [alembic.migration] Running upgrade 019 -> 020, remove redandunt progress ops
```

4. Neutron will be used accordingly. To do so, add the following line in the /etc/sahara/sahara.conf file:

   use-neutron=true

5. Add to the `sahara.conf` file the generated keystone admin parameters shown previously:

```
os_admin_username=admin
os_admin_password=198768b7617434823
os_admin_tenant_name=admin
os_auth_host=10.10.10.47
os_auth_port=5000
```

6. Create a new service entry in Keystone for Sahara named `Sahara`:

```
# keystone service-create --name=Sahara --type=Data-Processing
--description="Elastic Data Processing"
```

7. Create a new endpoint entry in Keystone for Sahara:

```
# keystone endpoint-create \
    --service sahara \
    --publicurl "http:// cc.pp:8386/v1.1/%(tenant_id)s" \
    --adminurl "http:// cc.pp:8386/v1.1/%(tenant_id)s" \
    --internalurl "http:// cc.pp:8386/v1.1/%(tenant_id)s"
```

8. By default, Sahara handles traffic on port `8386`. To enable traffic going through the Sahara service, add the following IPTable rules in the cloud controller node:

```
# nano /etc/sysconfig/iptables
-A INPUT -p tcp -m multiport --dports 8386 -j ACCEPT
```

9. Restart the IPTable service:

```
# systemctl restart iptables
```

10. Optionally, instruct the cloud controller node to start Sahara services on boot:

```
# systemctl enable openstack-sahara-all
```

Installing the Sahara user interface

The following steps describe how to integrate Sahara in the Horizon dashboard.

1. On the cloud controller node, install the `python-django-sahara` package:

```
# yum install python-django-sahara -y
```

2. Once installed, edit the OpenStack dashboard configuration file, which can be found in `/usr/share/openstack-dashboard/openstack_dashboard/settings.py`:

```
HORIZON_CONFIG = {
        'dashboards': ('nova','syspanel','settings',...,'sahara')
```

3. In the same file, add to the `INSTALLED_APPS` section the following line:

```
INSTALLED_APPS = (

    ...

    'saharadashboard',

    ...
```

4. Additionally, make sure to specify the usage of Neutron as the OpenStack's networking service by adding the following parameter in `/usr/share/openstack-dashboard/openstack_dashboard/local/local_settings.py`:

```
SAHARA_USE_NEUTRON=True
```

5. In the same file, add the Sahara URL and its corresponding port number as follows:

```
SAHARA_URL='http://10.10.10.47:8386/v1.1'
```

6. The next step requires restarting the `httpd` service as follows:

```
# systemctl restart httpd
```

7. Now, start the Sahara service and browse to the OpenStack dashboard:

```
# systemctl start openstack-sahara-api
```

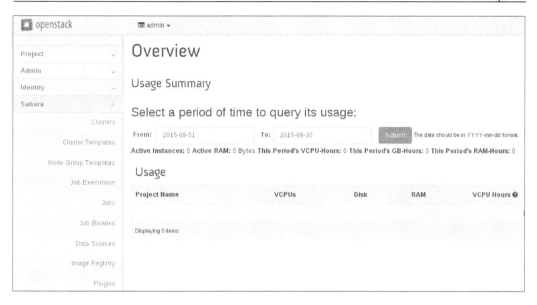

It is also possible to check via the Sahara CLI the correctness of the Sahara component installation. For example, run the following command line on the cloud controller node to list the default Sahara plugins:

```
# sahara plugin-list
```

```
+---------+---------------------+------------------------------+
| name    | versions            | title                        |
+---------+---------------------+------------------------------+
| cdh     | 5, 5.3.0, 5.4.0     | Cloudera Plugin              |
| hdp     | 2.0.6               | Hortonworks Data Platform    |
| spark   | 1.3.1, 1.0.0        | Apache Spark                 |
| vanilla | 2.6.0, 2.7.1        | Vanilla Apache Hadoop        |
+---------+---------------------+------------------------------+
```

The Sahara client provides several commands that can be used to create, delete, update, list, and edit clusters, images, job binaries, and data sources for the data processing API in the OpenStack environment. More details about the usage of these commands will be covered in subsequent chapters of this book.

Summary

In this chapter, we have installed OpenStack using the Packstack tool. Sahara has been successfully integrated and it is possible to instruct the Elastic Data Processing component in OpenStack using either the command-line interface or via Horizon.

Before walking through the rest of the chapters, it might be essential to have the OpenStack environment up and running without any issues. As has been described in *Chapter 1, The Essence of Big Data in the Cloud*, the Sahara service depends on other services and components of OpenStack. To run a Hadoop cluster, spin nodes, and run jobs, different services in OpenStack are involved. This will be covered in more detail in the next chapter, where we will examine the workflow of creating a Hadoop cluster in OpenStack using Sahara.

3
Using OpenStack Sahara

In the previous chapter, we have brought the OpenStack environment up and running. The Sahara project has been included and is ready to be used. In this chapter, we will start using Sahara to create a Hadoop cluster. Of course, running an Apache Hadoop cluster on top of OpenStack might require few planning considerations. This can include what type of instances will be assigned to the Hadoop cluster, image types, network setup, and storage backend. The following points will be highlighted:

- Understanding node types in Sahara for a Hadoop cluster
- Preparing an image for Hadoop nodes
- Configuring a network for a Hadoop cluster
- Creating and managing a Hadoop cluster using CLI
- Creating and managing a Hadoop cluster using Horizon

Planning a Hadoop deployment

Basically, a cluster defines a set of networked nodes or instances that work together. The building blocks in Hadoop clustering terminology can be categorized as Master and Slaves nodes. Each category will run a specific number of daemons to store data and run parallel computations tasks on all this data (MapReduce). The cluster nodes can assign different roles, which can be identified as the following:

- **NameNode**: This is the orchestrator and centerpiece of the Hadoop cluster, which stores the filesystem metadata.
- **JobTracker**: This is where the parallel data processing occurs using MapReduce.

- **DataNode**: This role can be assigned to the majority of Slave nodes that present the horse-worker of the cluster. It might be presumed that a data node daemon is a slave to the name node.

- **TaskTracker**: Like data node, this role can be assigned to a slave node as well. A task tracker daemon is a slave to the job tracker node.

 With YARN Hadoop V2, there are a few changes from an architectural level using other naming conventions, which are out of the scope of this book. To read more about the difference between Hadoop V2 and older versions, please check this out: `https://hadoop.apache.org/docs/r2.5.2/hadoop-yarn/hadoop-yarn-site/YARN.html`

Assigning Hadoop nodes

Depending on how many nodes you plan to set up in the Hadoop cluster, it might be easier using Sahara to mix roles as much as you want. Most importantly, all the roles should be present in a given cluster. A best practice is to simplify the deployment of the cluster by classifying the cited roles in a node group.

For example, the next illustration compels the **JobTracker** and **NameNode** in a node group called Master node group.

The **TaskTracker** and **DataNode** can run in the same slave node and be classified to a node group called Slave node group.

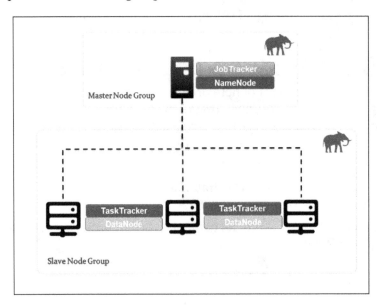

This role configuration setup may face huge performance problems and it is recommended to run a wider Hadoop cluster with more node groups in a production environment. This becomes trivial when data processed increases at sudden peaks.

Sahara provisioning plugins

At the time of writing this book, different provisioning plugins have been integrated into the Sahara project. Depending on which data processing framework you intend to use, the following table resumes the different provisioning plugins offered by Sahara and their correspondent deployment distribution use case:

Sahara plugin	Distribution deployment platform
Vanilla	Vanilla Apache Hadoop
Spark	Apache Spark
Cloudera	Cloudera Hadoop
HDP	Hortonworks Data Platform
MapR Distribution	MapR File System

The first example in this chapter will demonstrate how to create and deploy a Hadoop cluster using the Sahara Vanilla plugin.

 Chapter 5, Discovering Advanced Features with Sahara, covers more details on other plugins existing in the Sahara project.

Let's examine what makes a real shift in the architecture level of Apache Hadoop.

Hadoop version 2.x introduces a new layer named **YARN** (short for **Yet Another Resource Negotiator**) for cluster management. The hallmark of this shift is to leverage the processing data control of the cluster resource. With YARN, it might be possible to interact with data, for example by streaming Apache Storm or by means of batch scripts using MapReduce. On top of YARN, a variety of applications can be vectored like event processing using Apache Storm or SQL queries interaction by means of Apache Tez.

Depending on the OpenStack Sahara version you have installed, checking the right plugin version is essential for successful cluster deployment. Eventually, using Vanilla Apache Hadoop plugin 2.x will introduce slight responsibilities changes on node roles in the cluster. The JobTracker and TaskTracker split in different entities as follows:

- **ResourceManager**: By the means of a scheduler, the ResourceManager allocates resources among applications in the cluster

- **NodeManager**: The worker node in the cluster that launches containers of applications and keeps monitoring all resources to report them back for update to ResourceManager

- **ApplicationMaster**: This works in tandem with the ResouceManager and NodeManager entities to negotiate resources and execute tasks in the worker nodes

> You can find new updates of the last stable release of Apache Hadoop 2.x.x and its latest improvements at the following link: `https://hadoop.apache.org/docs/stable/`

Eventually, the JobTracker and TaskTracker entities will not be assigned using the Sahara Vanilla plugin 2.x.x in the next part of the chapter. Apache Hadoop 2.7.1 will be installed. The new role assignment for Hadoop processes can be implemented as the following:

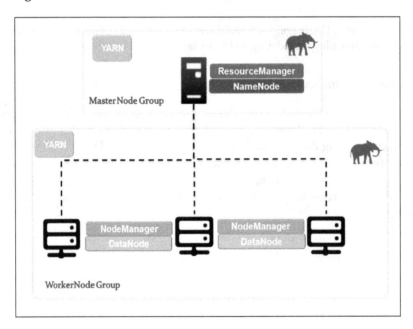

Creating a Hadoop cluster

To provision a Hadoop cluster, a prepared image should be uploaded or existing in Glance. We can start by uploading the image.

Preparing the image from Horizon

To avoid any compatibility issues during installation, it might be required to upload the supported image for the specific plugin. A very fast way is to download prepared images from the OpenStack upstream hosted by Mirantis as the following:

```
# wget http://sahara-files.mirantis.com/images/upstream/liberty/sahara-
liberty-vanilla-2.7.1-centos-7.qcow2
```

It is possible to build a customized image using the diskimage-builder tool.

 For more information on how to build a specific image, check the following link:

https://github.com/openstack/diskimage-builder

To register an image in Sahara, it is required that the image should be uploaded in the glance images catalog. From the **Sahara** tab in Horizon, click on **Image Registry**. By clicking on the **Register Image** button, the next wizard appears. The following settings are required to successfully register the image:

- Image name from the dropdown list.
- Default username of the cloud-init user. In our case, the username is **centos**.

- Tags are required by selecting the plugin version. It is also possible to mention more custom tags in order to differentiate between the Sahara images when registering them with a large number.

Preparing the image using CLI

The next step requires uploading the download image using the glance command line:

```
# glance image-create --name=pp-sahara-vanilla-2.7.1-centos7 --disk-
format=qcow2 -container=bare < sahara-liberty-vanilla-2.7.1-centos-7.
qcow2
```

```
+-----------------------+-------------------------------------------+
| Property              | Value                                     |
+-----------------------+-------------------------------------------+
| checksum              | 142c667e296b0a1150ee98ae87218b35          |
| container_format      | bare                                      |
| created_at            | 2015-10-30T13:38:52Z                      |
| disk_format           | qcow2                                     |
| id                    | 49fa54c0-18c0-4292-aa61-fa1a56dbfd24      |
| min_disk              | 0                                         |
| min_ram               | 0                                         |
| name                  | pp-sahara--vanilla-2.7.1-centos7          |
| owner                 | 24c98423219148a1a6f8cd947a627aeb          |
| protected             | False                                     |
| size                  | 1362165760                                |
| status                | active                                    |
| tags                  | []                                        |
| updated_at            | 2015-10-30T13:40:11Z                      |
| virtual_size          | None                                      |
| visibility            | private                                   |
+-----------------------+-------------------------------------------+
```

The following command line will instruct glance to register the uploaded image in Sahara. To register an image using the Sahara command line, use the following syntax:

```
# sahara image-register --id <image_id> [--username <name>]
[--description <desc>]
```

Where:

--id: is the image ID of the glance image. It can be obtained using the image-list command line

--username: Any image built or downloaded should have a privileged user in the image

--description: Additional information of the image

It is possible to export the image ID into shell for later usage as the following:

```
# export IMAGE_ID=49fa54c0-18c0-4292-aa61-fa1a56dbfd24
# sahara image-register --id $IMAGE_ID --username centos
--description 'Sahara image CentOS 7 Hadoop Vanilla 2.7.1'
```

Using Vanilla might require a tagged image in the Sahara Image Registry. At the very least, the following tags should be added to the image: vanilla and x.x.x . The x.x.x. tag can refer to any Hadoop version.

To add a tag to a registered image in Sahara, use the following syntax:

```
# sahara image-add-tag [--name NAME] [--id <image_id>] --tag <tag>
```

Where:

--NAME: The name of the image existing in glance.

--id: is the image ID of the glance image. It can be obtained using the glance image-list command line.

--tag: Tag string.

In our example, we are going to add vanilla, 2.7.1, and pp_test tags. This can be done easily via the Sahara command line or via Horizon:

```
# sahara image-add-tag --name pp-sahara--vanilla-2.7.1-centos7 --id
$IMAGE_ID --tag vanilla
# sahara image-add-tag --name pp-sahara--vanilla-2.7.1-centos7 --id
$IMAGE_ID --tag 2.7.1
# sahara image-add-tag --name pp-sahara--vanilla-2.7.1-centos7 --id
$IMAGE_ID --tag pp_test
```

We check in the Sahara tab images in Horizon if it is successfully registered and tagged, as illustrated in the next graphic:

Image Overview

Information

Name	pp-sahara--vanilla-2.7.1-centos7
ID	49fa54c0-18c0-4292-aa61-fa1a56dbfd24
Owner	24c98423219148a1a6f8cd947a627aeb
Status	Active
Public	No
Protected	No
Checksum	142c667e296b0a1150ee98ae87218b35
Created	Oct. 30, 2015, 1:38 p.m.
Updated	Oct. 30, 2015, 1:45 p.m.

Specs

Size	1.3 GB
Container Format	BARE
Disk Format	QCOW2

Custom Properties

_sahara_description	Sahara Image CentOS 7 Hadoop Vanilla 2.7.1
_sahara_tag_2.7.1	True
_sahara_tag_pp_test	True
_sahara_tag_vanilla	True
_sahara_username	centos

Creating the Node Group Template

The Node Group Template in Sahara is a concept intended to configure a set of instances that have the same configuration and properties such as RAM and CPU.

Creating the Node Group Template in Horizon

The creation of the Node Group Template using the dashboard is straightforward. From the **Sahara** tab, click on **Node Group Templates**, then a simple click on **Create Template** will ask us to specify the first Node Group Template. The first window in the wizard exposes the **Plugin Name** and its **Version**. In our example, the vanilla plugins **Version** is **2.7.1**.

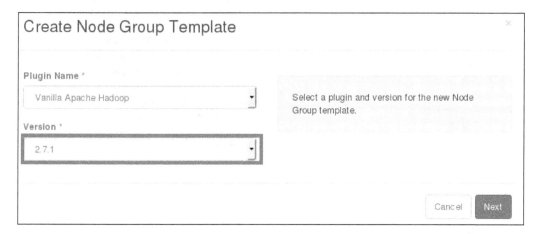

The first template will be dedicated to the Master nodes as the following:

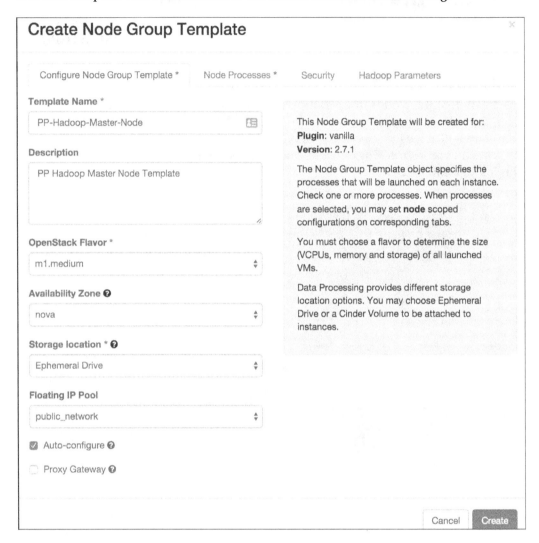

Note that Node Processes in Hadoop 2.x will be different than the ones specified in Hadoop 1.x. Thus, the master node can be assigned to run **namenode, secondarynamenode, resourcemanager**, and optionally **historyserver** as the **MapReduce process**.

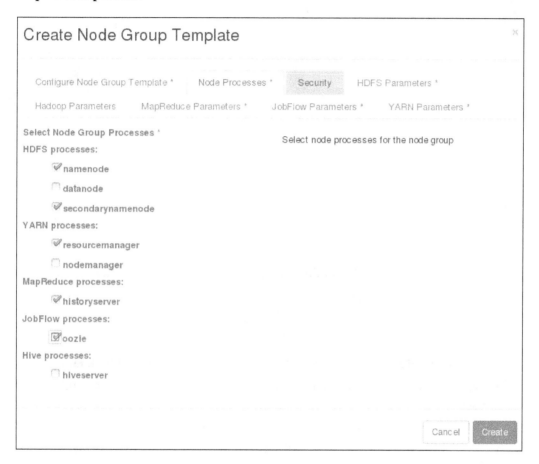

We can keep the default **Security Groups** in the next **Security** tab in the dashboard. It might be recommended to create in advance the needed **Security Groups** in OpenStack and associated within the template for security preferences.

The next **HDFS Parameters** tab defines the different options of an instance of HDFS.

When running a Hadoop job, the binaries will be moved from the node local filesystem to HDFS. Refining the following set of parameters in a larger Hadoop deployment with more complex jobs is essential:

- **dfs.datanode.handler.count**: How many server threads for the datanode
- **dfs.datanode.du.reserved**: How much of the available disk space will not be taken into account for HDFS use
- **dfs.namenode.handler.count**: How many server threads for the namenode
- **dfs.datanode.failed.volumes.tolerated**: How many volumes are allowed to fail before a datanode instance stops
- **dfs.datanode.max.transfer.threads**: What is the maximum number of threads to be used in order to transfer data to/from the DataNode instance
- **SecondaryNameNode Heap Size**: How much memory will be assigned to the heap size of the handle workload per SecondaryNode instance
- **NameNode Heap Size**: How much memory will be assigned to the heap size of the handle workload per NameNode instance
- **DataNode Heap Size**: How much memory will be assigned to the heap size of the handle workload per DataNode instance

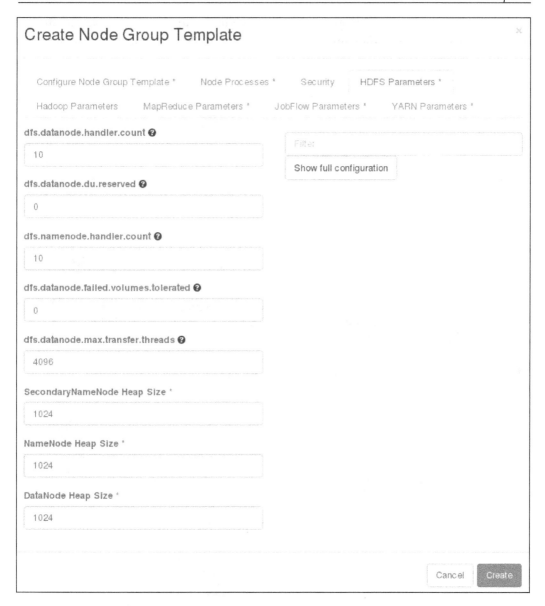

Once the master template is created and ready, we can move forward to create a template for the worker cluster.

Like the master template node group, click on **Node Group Template** and **Create Template**. The same Vanilla Hadoop plugin version must be used, which in our case is **Vanilla Apache Hadoop** version **2.7.1**.

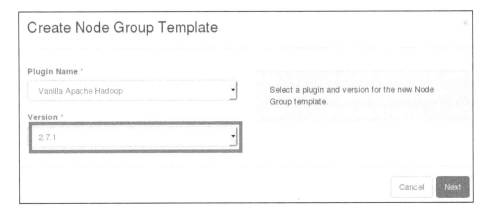

 Using master and worker node groups with different Vanilla Apache Hadoop versions will generate a version compatibility error when creating the cluster.

The next figure illustrates the general parameters template for the worker group nodes:

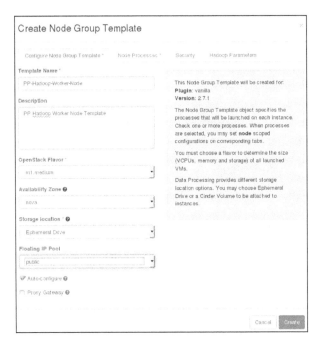

The node processes in the worker group are simpler than the master nodes. Remember that Node Processes in Hadoop 2.x will be different than the ones specified in Hadoop 1.x. Thus, the worker node can be assigned to run datanode and nodemanager processes.

Create Node Group Template

Configure Node Group Template *   Node Processes *   Security   HDFS Parameters *

Hadoop Parameters   YARN Parameters *

Select Node Group Processes *

HDFS processes:

☐ namenode

☑ datanode

☐ secondarynamenode

YARN processes:

☐ resourcemanager

☑ nodemanager

MapReduce processes:

☐ historyserver

JobFlow processes:

☐ oozie

Hive processes:

☐ hiveserver

Select node processes for the node group

Cancel   Create

We can keep the default values for the rest of the tabs.

From Horizon, it might be possible to see both Master and Worker Template nodes created successfully.

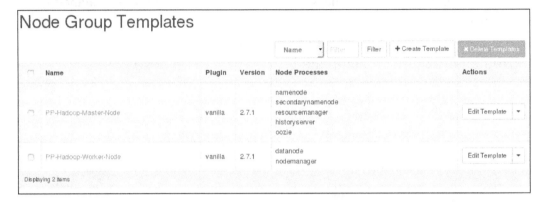

Creating a Node Group Template using CLI

It is also possible to use the Sahara CLI to create and update Node Group Templates, which simply need the correct file syntax in JSON format.

To create a master node group template, create a new file called `master_template_pp.json` with the following content:

```
# nano master_template_pp.json
{
    "name": "Master-PP-Template",
    "flavor_id": "2",
    "plugin_name": "vanilla",
    "hadoop_version": "2.7.1",
    "node_processes": ["namenode", "secondarynamenode"
    ,"resourcemanager", "historyserver", "oozie"],
    "auto_security_group": true
}
```

Next, upload the new template file using the Sahara CLI as the following:

```
# sahara node-group-template-create --json master_template_pp.json
```

```
Property                      | Value
volume_local_to_instance      | False
volumes_availability_zone     | None
availability_zone             | None
volume_mount_prefix           | /volumes/disk
plugin_name                   | vanilla
floating_ip_pool              | None
is_default                    | False
volumes_size                  | 0
use_autoconfig                | True
is_proxy_gateway              | False
volumes_per_node              | 0
is_public                     | False
hadoop_version                | 2.7.1
id                            | 53ed88e9-9f7f-43ab-a595-73a00a2ed630
security_groups               | None
name                          | Master-PP-Template
tenant_id                     | 24c98423219148a1a6f8cd947a627aeb
created_at                    | 2015-10-30T16:11:41
volume_type                   | None
is_protected                  | False
node_configs                  | {}
flavor_id                     | 2
node_processes                | namenode, secondarynamenode, resourcemanager, historyserver, oozie
auto_security_group           | True
```

To create a worker node group template, create a new file called `worker_template_pp.json` with the following content:

```
# nano worker_template_pp.json
{
 " name": "PP-Worker-Template",
  "flavor_id": "2",
  "plugin_name": "vanilla",
  "hadoop_version": "2.7.1",
  "node_processes": ["nodemanager", "datanode"],
  "auto_security_group": true
}
```

Next, upload the new template file using the Sahara CLI as the following:

```
# sahara node-group-template-create --json worker_template_pp.json
```

```
+------------------------------+--------------------------------------+
| Property                     | Value                                |
+------------------------------+--------------------------------------+
| volume_local_to_instance     | False                                |
| volumes_availability_zone    | None                                 |
| availability_zone            | None                                 |
| volume_mount_prefix          | /volumes/disk                        |
| plugin_name                  | vanilla                              |
| floating_ip_pool             | None                                 |
| is_default                   | False                                |
| volumes_size                 | 0                                    |
| use_autoconfig               | True                                 |
| is_proxy_gateway             | False                                |
| volumes_per_node             | 0                                    |
| is_public                    | False                                |
| hadoop_version               | 2.7.1                                |
| id                           | 2c0ba50f-5e93-4948-a4c9-39f29ef372ed |
| security_groups              | None                                 |
| name                         | PP-Worker-Template                   |
| tenant_id                    | 24c98423219148a1a6f8cd947a627aeb     |
| created_at                   | 2015-10-30T16:12:47                  |
| volume_type                  | None                                 |
| is_protected                 | False                                |
| node_configs                 | {}                                   |
| flavor_id                    | 2                                    |
| node_processes               | nodemanager, datanode                |
| auto_security_group          | True                                 |
+------------------------------+--------------------------------------+
```

It might be possible to list the created node groups cluster template as the following:

```
# sahara node-group-template-list
```

```
| name              | id                                   | plugin_name | node_processes                                                    |
| Master-PP-Template | 53ed68e9-9f7f-43ab-e595-73a00a2ed630 | vanilla     | namenode, secondarynamenode, resourcemanager, historyserver, oozie |
| PP-Worker-Template | 2c0ba50f-5e93-4948-a4c9-39f29ef372ed | vanilla     | nodemanager, datanode                                            |
```

Creating the Node Cluster Template

In order to instruct Sahara to run a fully Hadoop cluster by the means of master and worker cluster groups, it might be required to merge the templates newly created in a single one that will contain the entire configuration that describes the entire Hadoop cluster. The next part will cover how to create a cluster template.

Creating the Node Cluster Template with Horizon

From the **Sahara** tab in Horizon, click on **Cluster Templates**, then a simple click on **Create Template** will ask us to specify **Cluster Template** details. The first window in the wizard exposes the **Plugin name** and its version. In our example, the vanilla plugins version used is **2.7.1**.

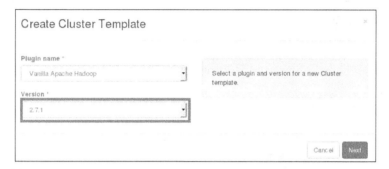

The next step of the wizard will specify general details of the cluster such as the name and an overall description of the cluster template. The same tab gives the means to specify a certain list of processes to run in affinity groups, which will be covered in more detail in *Chapter 5, Discovering Advanced Features with Sahara.*

The next tab makes it possible to easily mix and assign roles for nodes. Since we have created only two different group nodes, the Select a Node Group Template drop-down list exposes only node groups that have been created previously. It is a very simple and flexible way to add nodes as much as needed to start deploying the cluster using the Count **+** and **-** for each node group added:

The next tab specifies general HDFS settings for the overall cluster as the following:

- **dfs.permissions.enabled**: If checked, permission checking in HDFS will be enabled

- **dfs.replication**: Defines the default block replication value

- **dfs.replication.max**: Defines the maximum number of block replication

- **dfs.namenode.replication.min**: Defines the minimum number of block replication

- **dfs.blocksize**: Defines the default block size for the new files in bytes

 The **dfs.blocksize** value can be a more human readable suffix format such as k for kilobytes, m for megabytes, g for gigabytes, t for terabytes, p for petabytes, and e for exabytes.

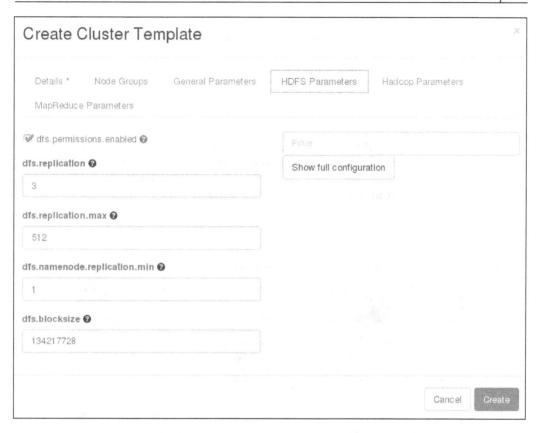

Creating the Node Cluster Template using CLI

Using the Sahara CLI, creating a Node Cluster Template is fairly simple. Create a new file called `master_template_pp.json` with the following content:

```
# nano pp-hadoop-cluster-template.json
{
    "name": "pp- hadoop-cluster-template",
    "plugin_name": "vanilla",
    "hadoop_version": "2.7.1",
    "node_groups": [
        {
            "name": "master",
            "node_group_template_id": "53ed88e9-9f7f-43ab-a595-
            73a00a2ed630",
            "count": 1
        },
        {
```

```
        "name": "workers",
        "node_group_template_id": "2c0ba50f-5e93-4948-a4c9-
        39f29ef372ed",
        "count": 2
    }
  ]
}
```

The previous JSON file exposes the `node_groups` attribute that defines the defined node groups created previously. Sahara will need to specify them by the means of ID, which is denoted by the `node_group_template_id` attribute. To get the corresponding node group IDs, use the `sahara node-group-template-list` command line.

Next, upload the new template file using the Sahara CLI as the following:

```
# sahara node-group-template-create --json master_template_pp.json
```

```
+-----------------------------+--------------------------------------+
| Property                    | Value                                |
+-----------------------------+--------------------------------------+
| description                 | None                                 |
| updated_at                  | None                                 |
| plugin_name                 | vanilla                              |
| is_default                  | False                                |
| use_autoconfig              | True                                 |
| anti_affinity               | []                                   |
| node_groups                 | workers: 2; master: 1                |
| is_public                   | False                                |
| hadoop_version              | 2.7.1                                |
| id                          | 60524c6c-bea0-4065-bb7a-56f24ed91357 |
| neutron_management_network  | None                                 |
| name                        | pp-hadoop-cluster-template           |
| cluster_configs             | {}                                   |
| created_at                  | 2015-10-30T16:17:18                  |
| default_image_id            | None                                 |
| shares                      | None                                 |
| is_protected                | False                                |
| tenant_id                   | 24c98423219148a1a6f8cd947a627aeb     |
+-----------------------------+--------------------------------------+
```

Launching the Hadoop cluster

The last step of the Hadoop wizard deployment will simply instruct Sahara to provision the cluster.

Launching the Hadoop cluster with Horizon

Navigate to the **Sahara** tab in Horizon and click on the **Clusters** panel. Next, click the **Launch Cluster** button. This will ask us to choose the plugin name and version. In our case, we keep the same Vanilla plugin and version **2.7.1**.

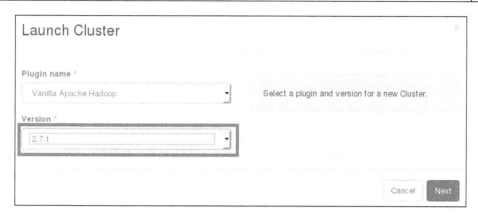

The next tab is much simpler: it is required just to specify a name for the cluster, select the cluster template from the dropdown list, and the base image already registered in Sahara. Note that the **Keypair** will be needed when it requires authenticating to the cluster instances. On the other hand, within the new versions of Sahara, it might be required to specify the neutron management network since Sahara was configured to use the Neutron service. This will enable the instances when getting provisioned to have fixed IP addresses on the specific network segment.

The following screen capture shows the cluster created:

	Name	Plugin	Version	Status
	PP-Hadoop-Cluster	vanilla	2.7.1	Starting

Launching the Hadoop cluster using the CLI

Before creating a JSON file that defines the launching cluster, it might be needed in the first place to gather information regarding the cluster template ID, the image ID, and the neutron management network ID. The following command lines will help us to collect the needed pieces of information:

- glance image ID:

```
# sahara image-list
```

- cluster template ID:

```
# sahara cluster -list
```

- neutron management network ID:

```
# neutron net-list
```

Next, create a new JSON file to launch the cluster using the information cited previously:

```
# nano pp_launch_cluster.json
  {
    "name": "pp-launch-cluster",
    "plugin_name": "vanilla",
    "hadoop_version": "2.7.1",
    "cluster_template_id" : "60524c6c-bea0-4065-bb7a-
    56f24ed91357",
    "default_image_id": "49fa54c0-18c0-4292-aa61-fa1a56dbfd24"
    "neutron_management_network": "4f9d08d2-80d5-485a-a601-
    e4135caf2eda"
  }
```

Now, to launch the cluster it needs only to use the following command line:

```
# sahara cluster-create --json pp_launch_cluster.json
```

Summary

Provisioning a Hadoop cluster using Sahara in OpenStack is not a complex task anymore. Sahara is very rich in terms of plugins and versioning. Although the chapter has covered only the Hadoop Vanilla plugin, it might be possible to run other types of clusters by going through the same steps using a different plugin of your choice. The beauty of Sahara is the simplicity of the workflow of a complete Hadoop cluster up and running using Horizon or via the CLI. After creating and launching your first Hadoop cluster, it is time to discover the other side of Sahara: running jobs, which will be the topic of the next chapter.

4
Executing Jobs with Sahara

In the preceding chapter, we looked at how a Hadoop cluster can be created in OpenStack by means of templates. In this chapter, we will use the cluster by running and executing Hadoop jobs efficiently. Keep in mind that running jobs in Sahara depends on the choice of **Elastic Data Processing** (**EDP**) provisioning plugin discussed in the previous chapter. Thus, this chapter will guide you through the following points:

- Understanding the essential components to run an EDP job in Sahara
- Discussing the data source workflow in Sahara
- Configuring a job in Sahara
- Gathering the pieces together by executing a job in Sahara using Horizon
- Enhancing EDP in Sahara using REST APIs
- Executing a Spark job using the Sahara REST API

Job glossary in Sahara

Elastic Data Processing functionality exposed by Sahara simplifies enormously the execution of any task or job in a defined Hadoop cluster. Now, when we have a running big data cluster on OpenStack, it is possible to burst workload and check results.

To run a job in Sahara, several objects must be provided before executing a job as the following:

- Data localization: Path of input/output data
- Code: Defines which code will be executed and run

It is important to decide the first place where Sahara should grab data to start processing it and where it will store results. The next diagram shows a sample overview of data sources using Swift within Sahara:

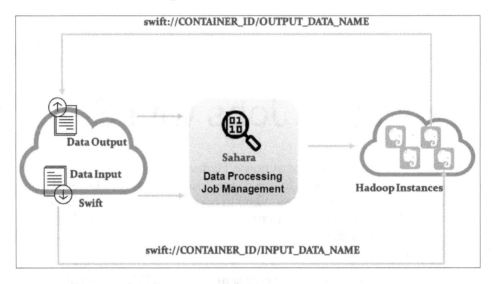

Data localization can be optionally configured in Sahara using one of the following storage types:

- **Swift**: OpenStack object storage
- **HDFS**: Native Hadoop Distributed File System storage
- **Manila**: Network filesystem shares in OpenStack

Job binaries in Sahara

Another essential element to execute a job in Sahara is the job binary. This is where scripts, JAR files, and file credentials will be referenced. The job binary stores locally scripts or JAR files using Sahara's own database, or externally using Swift or Manila. The paths of scripts and JAR files are referenced by means of the URL.

> Manila is a new incubated project in OpenStack providing a file-sharing service for the cloud introduced in the Kilo OpenStack release. Unlike Swift and Cinder, Manila enables the mapping of external storage systems using file-based protocols such as NAS using NFS or SMB to the instances running in OpenStack.

The next table shows a few requirements for job binaries storage options in Sahara:

	Storage type	Access	Authentication
Internal	Sahara database	Sahara cluster	Sahara credentials
Swift	Object storage	Swift proxy	Swift credentials
Manila	File-shared storage	Mounted shares	Share access control

Jobs in Sahara

In the OpenStack Liberty release, many jobs types are supported by Sahara as follows:

- **Java**: Executes jobs from a Java action in a specific Hadoop workflow such as Oozie.

- **Hive**: Queries data in a Hadoop cluster using HiveQL language. Hive converts a HiveQL query into a Java MapReduce program before submitting the results into the Hadoop cluster.

- **MapReduce**: Splits the input data into different and independents chunks. The split data will be processed by the map tasks in a parallel fashion and output to the reduce tasks.

- **MapReduce.Streaming**: Allows a MapReduce program to be written in different dynamic programming languages by passing data between the Map and the Reduce codes by means of STDIN (standard input) and STDOUT (standard output).

- **Pig**: Uses the Pig Latin language that specifies dataflow pipelines to query data in a Hadoop cluster. Pig generates a MapReduce code from the Pig Latin scripts.

- **Shell**: Executes a shell script through a Hadoop framework such as Oozie.

- **Spark**: Allows running multi-step data pipelines so different jobs can work with the same data.

Running jobs in Sahara

In the previous chapter, we had a running Hadoop cluster with one Master and three Worker nodes on top of OpenStack. Be aware that running any job type in Sahara requires an Active state of the provisioned cluster.

Executing jobs via Horizon

Since we intend to use Swift for input and output data, the first example will illustrate how to neaten a simple text file by trimming and removing space in each line. The text file looks like the following:

```
        OpenStack
EDP
    Sahara
        Swift
Jobs
```

To do so, we will execute a Pig Job in the Sahara cluster and designate the location of the text file in Swift named input. The Pig script might look like the following:

```
I = load '$INPUT' using PigStorage(':') as (cloud: chararray);
O = foreach I generate com.hadoopbook.pig.Trim(cloud);
store O into '$OUTPUT' USING PigStorage();
```

Let's take a look at doing a few steps in Horizon to execute a job in Sahara:

1. Under the **Object Store** tab, select **Containers**:

2. Click on **Create Container** to create a new container in Swift and name it pp-input.

3. The next step requires creating an object and uploading it to the created container in Swift by clicking on the **Upload Object** button as follows:

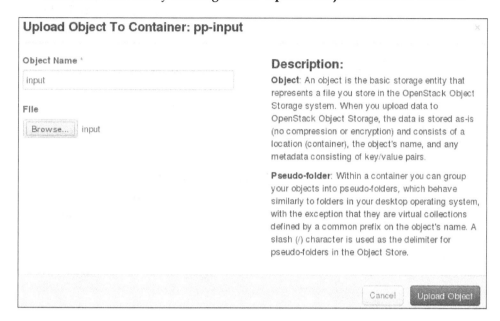

4. Check the new text file uploaded object in Swift:

5. At this stage, we have all the needed resources to start running jobs outside of the Sahara environment. Next, navigate to the **Sahara** tab and select **Data Source**. Sahara should locate where it can find the data input so the Pig process can manipulate them. Click on the **Create Data Source** button as the following:

The Swift URL has the following format:
`swift://<container_name.sahara>/<object_name>`
The Sahara Swift URLs might include a `.sahara` suffix.

The source username and password fields can be left by default. Both credentials parameters are configured from the Packstack installer.

To change both Swift source username/password, update the Swift configuration files on the controller node and reload the configuration.

6. Sahara will also need to locate where to store the results. Redo the previous step by changing the data source name and the Swift URL as the following:

Create Data Source

Create Data Source *

Name *

pp-data-output

Data Source Type *

Swift

URL *

swift:// input.sahara/output

Source username *

admin

Source password *

••••••••••••••••

Description

Create a Data Source with a specified name.

Select the type of your Data Source.

You may need to enter the username and password for your Data Source.

You may also enter an optional description for your Data Source.

7. Next, Sahara should be aware of the job binary location. To do so, select the **Job Binaries** tab and click on the **Create Job Binary** button as follows:

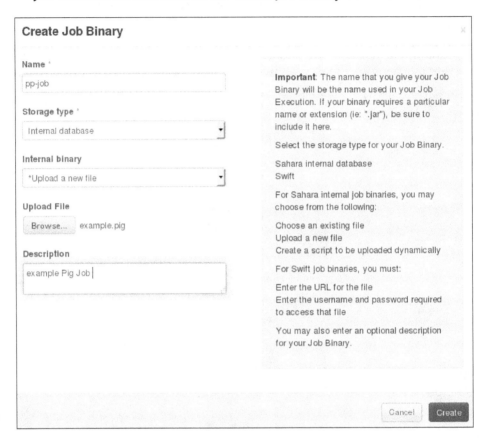

Create Job Binary

Name *

pp-job

Storage type *

Internal database

Internal binary

*Upload a new file

Upload File

Browse... example.pig

Description

example Pig Job

Important: The name that you give your Job Binary will be the name used in your Job Execution. If your binary requires a particular name or extension (ie: ".jar"), be sure to include it here.

Select the storage type for your Job Binary.

Sahara internal database
Swift

For Sahara internal job binaries, you may choose from the following:

Choose an existing file
Upload a new file
Create a script to be uploaded dynamically

For Swift job binaries, you must:

Enter the URL for the file
Enter the username and password required to access that file

You may also enter an optional description for your Job Binary.

Cancel   Create

8. Select the **Jobs** tab and click on the **Create Job** button. The next wizard looks as follows:

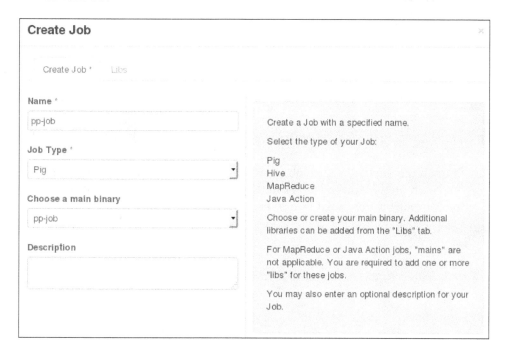

9. Note that Sahara provides different job types from the drop-down menu list:

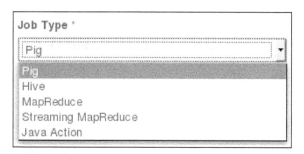

10. Optionally, it might be possible to upload additional libraries. For example, it might be necessary for other job types such as MapReduce and Java Action to provide at least one library through the second tab of the wizard:

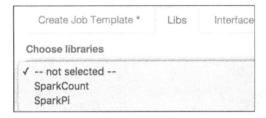

11. Launch the newly created job from the **Jobs** tab. Notice that executing the job on the created Hadoop cluster in the previous chapter can be chosen through the More drop-down list button as shown in the following:

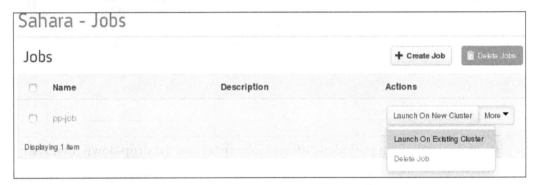

12. The final step will require selecting the **Input** and **Output** data sources and the **Cluster** name as follows:

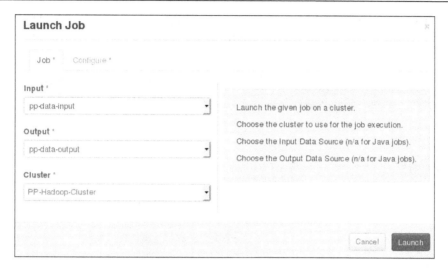

13. Launching the cluster will execute the job on the Hadoop cluster. The job execution progress shows the current status of the job in the cluster in the **Status** column in Horizon as the following:

14. The job can take a while depending on the designated task in the Hadoop cluster by changing its progress state from **Pending** to **Running**. To collect results from the Swift output, the job progress should end up with a **Succeeded** status. An additional cluster details check can be performed by browsing to the **Clusters** tab in Sahara. For example, HDFS web user interface can be accessed on the Hadoop master node on port 50070.

15. From the same cluster information tab, it is possible to access the HDFS NameNode web user interface; simply click on the exposed URL by Sahara as follows:

16. Accessing the YARN web user interface provides more details on running jobs in the Hadoop cluster, in our case Oozie:

Web UI: http://10.0.2.23:8088

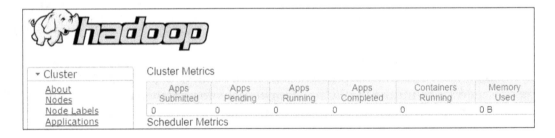

17. The job execution status should end with a **Succeeded** status as follows:

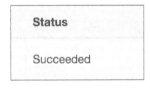

18. Job results can be collected by downloading data from the **Container** output in Swift:

19. The output data can be downloaded to be verified. The text file has the following content:

```
OpenStack
EDP
Sahara
Swift
Jobs
```

Executing jobs using the Sahara RESTful API

OpenStack provides within each service a rich RESTful API. This enables customizing access to the resources and provides more capabilities to manage the underlining components. The previous section explained how to run an EDP job using the web user interface. Note that automating such workflow is also possible using the Sahara REST API.

A REST API, or Representational State Transfer Application Programming Interface, is an approach of communications between components in a distributed system architecture (producer and consumer model). It is commonly used in cloud-based APIs. Typically, REST is designed to run over HTTP and exposes several architectural advantages such as the ability to leverage to a cache through a layered system, stateless, and decouples the producers from consumers. To read more about the Sahara REST API, check this out:

http://docs.openstack.org/developer/sahara/restapi/
rest_api_v1.1_EDP.html

API authentication

In order to interact with the Sahara API, a request must be sent to Keystone to get an authentication token. This can be achieved by sending the request to its public API. The obtained token will be provided to Sahara as part of the API call. Using the curl command line, this sequence can be illustrated as the following:

```
# curl -s -d '{"auth": {"tenantName": "admin", "passwordCredentials":
{"username" : "admin", "password": "5e185a8ced9e4858"}}}' -H 'Content-
Type: application/json'  http://os-cc.packtpub:5000/v2.0/tokens | python
-m json.tool
```

Each Sahara API request generates a JSON output. For a quick and efficient representation of the JSON output, it might be useful to redirect the output to the Python JSON formatting tool using `python -m json.tool` in the command line. This will valid a pretty print of the debug format.

The curl command line will submit a request to the OpenStack cloud controller to its specific authentication service URL, `http://os-cc.packtpub:5000/v2.0/tokens`. It is required to submit, for example, the required credentials provided by the `keystonadminrc` source file. In the previous example, we have only one `tenant` called `admin`. The end of the command line provided a better representation of the command output in JSON format as the following:

```
...
"token": {

        "audit_ids": [

            "yOXxKjFsQlGzHonMVAuBQQ"

        ],

        "expires": "2016-02-07T20:38:58Z",

        "id": "bc3243b3177141c3abc684d82db14051",

        "issued_at": "2016-02-07T19:38:58.657425",

        "tenant": {

            "description": "admin tenant",

            "enabled": true,

            "id": "f4af2ed9ba3c4c079edd02bb7809113d",

            "name": "admin"

        }

...
```

Obviously, the token section in the JSON output enables starting querying the Sahara API using `tenant id` and `auth` token highlighted in the previous command-line output. Make sure any request to the Sahara endpoint is pointed to its configured URL and port number. In our example, the Sahara port endpoint is `8386`. This parameter can be configured in the Sahara configuration file. A simple REST API request can be sent to Sahara end point as the following:

```
# curl -H "X-Auth-Token: bc3243b3177141c3abc684d82db14051" http:// os-cc.
packtpub:8386/ | python -m json.tool
{
    "versions": [
        {
            "id": "v1.0",
            "status": "SUPPORTED"
        },
        {
            "id": "v1.1",
            "status": "CURRENT"
        }
    ]
}
```

The previous output shows the API versions. At this time, the API version currently used is 1.1. The response shown earlier also supports version 1.0.

Launching an EDP job

In the next section, we will execute a simple job using the Sahara RESTful API. For this purpose, the authentication token and the token ID should be used along all the REST API calls. The next example will execute a simple elastic data processing job using the Spark plugin in Sahara. The job will be executed to read from an input text file stored in Swift and count the number of occurrence for each word. The result will be sorted in an output file stored locally. To execute successfully the Spark job, we will need to go through the following steps:

1. Upload and register a Spark image in Sahara.
2. Create Spark node groups templates.
3. Create a Spark cluster template.
4. Create a Spark job binary.
5. Create a Spark job template.
6. Execute the Spark job on the active Spark cluster and extract the results.

Registering a Spark image using REST API

A prepared Spark image can be downloaded from the Sahara images repository hosted by Mirantis as the following:

```
# wget http://sahara-files.mirantis.com/images/upstream/liberty/sahara-
liberty-spark-1.3.1-ubuntu-14.04.qcow2
```

The downloaded file is an Ubuntu image including Spark 1.3.1. The default username is `ubuntu`. *Chapter 5, Discovering Advanced Features with Sahara,* will discuss in more depth how to create customized images for different Sahara plugins.

On the OpenStack cloud controller, run the following API request command line, which will instruct the Sahara endpoint to register the downloaded Spark image:

```
# curl -g -H 'Content-Type: application/json' \

-H 'X-Auth-Token: bc3243b3177141c3abc684d82db14051' \

-H 'Accept: application/json' \

-X POST \

http://os-cc.packtpub:8386/v1.1/f4af2ed9ba3c4c079edd02bb7809113d/

images/026e348a-d0ac-4e38-9192-436277abba9e \

-d '{"username": "ubuntu", "description":"Spark 1.3.1"}' | python -m
json.tool
```

It is important to provide the ID of the image from Glance. In our example, `026e348a-d0ac-4e38-9192-436277abba9e` is the ID of the Spark image added to Glance.

> To register an image using the Sahara API, use the POST method by providing both the Tenant ID and Image ID within the following format
>
> `/v1.1/<TENANT_ID>/images/<IMAGE_ID>`

The output of the command line should generate a detailed description of the image as the following:

```
{
    "image":{
        "status":"ACTIVE",
        "username":"ubuntu",
        "updated":"2016-02-20T18:42:46Z",
        "OS-EXT-IMG-SIZE:size":957378048,
        "name":"Spark",
```

```
    "created":"2016-02-16T04:51:09Z",
    "tags":[

    ],
    "minDisk":0,
    "progress":100,
    "minRam":0,
    "metadata":{
        "_sahara_username":"ubuntu",
        "_sahara_description":"Spark 1.3.1"
    },
    "id":"026e348a-d0ac-4e38-9192-436277abba9e",
    "description":"Spark 1.3.1"
    }
}
```

As was mentioned in *Chapter 3, Using OpenStack Sahara*, each registered image in Sahara needs to be tagged. In our example, the new uploaded image can have the following tags: 'spark' and '1.3.1'. Using the Sahara API, we can add the mentioned tags as the following:

```
# curl -g -H 'Content-Type: application/json' \
-H 'X-Auth-Token: bc3243b3177141c3abc684d82db14051 ' \
-H 'Accept: application/json' \
-X POST\
http://os-cc.packtpub:8386/v1.1/f4af2ed9ba3c4c079edd02bb7809113d/
images/026e348a-d0ac-4e38-9192-436277abba9e/tag \
-d '{"tags": ["spark","1.3.1"]}' | python -m json.tool
```

The next extract of the output of the previous REST API request validates the success of the Curl command line:

```
...
"tags": [
            "1.3.1",
            "spark"
        ],
...
```

To add tags to an image using the Sahara API, use the POST method by providing both the Tenant ID and Image ID within the following format:
`/v1.1/<TENANT_ID>/images/<IMAGE_ID>/tag`

Creating Spark node group templates

The next step requires the creation of two different Spark node group templates. The first template will assemble the `master` and `namenode` roles as the following:

```
# curl -g -H 'Content-Type: application/json' \
-H 'X-Auth-Token: bc3243b3177141c3abc684d82db14051 ' \
-H 'Accept: application/json' \
-X POST http://os-cc.packtpub:8386/v1.1/
f4af2ed9ba3c4c079edd02bb7809113d/node-group-templates \
-d '{
    "plugin_name": "spark",
    "hadoop_version": "1.3.1",
    "node_processes": [
        "master",
        "namenode"
    ],
    "name": "PP-Spark-Master-Node",
    "floating_ip_pool": "fbf94e05-3d97-48c2-83c4-a77a0d2ffea0",
    "flavor_id": "2"
}' | python -m json.tool
```

The POST request also includes the ID of the flavor from OpenStack (`m1.small`) as well as the floating IP Pool ID (Public Network). This will enable access to the Spark instances in the next steps to collect results locally. An extract of a successful run of the previous API request can be shown as the following:

```
"node_group_template": {
        "auto_security_group": false,
        "availability_zone": null,
        "created_at": "2016-02-20T19:10:53",
        "flavor_id": "2",
        "floating_ip_pool": "fbf94e05-3d97-48c2-83c4-a77a0d2ffea0",
        "hadoop_version": "1.3.1",
```

```
        "id": "f0c833ec-53d5-4a29-8381-8da20c4df707",
        "is_default": false,
        "is_protected": false,
        "is_proxy_gateway": false,
        "is_public": false,
        "name": "PP-Spark-Master-Node",
        "node_configs": {},
        "node_processes": [
            "master",
            "namenode"
        ],
        "plugin_name": "spark",
...
```

Likewise, a second node group template should exist that will assemble `slave` and `datanode` Spark roles. Similar to the `PP-Spark-Master-Node` node group template created previously, create a new `PP-Spark-Slave-Node` group template as follows:

```
# curl -g -H 'Content-Type: application/json' \
-H 'X-Auth-Token: bc3243b3177141c3abc684d82db14051 ' \
-H 'Accept: application/json' \
-X POST http://os-cc.packtpub:8386/v1.1/
f4af2ed9ba3c4c079edd02bb7809113d/node-group-templates \
-d '{
    "plugin_name": "spark",
    "hadoop_version": "1.3.1",
    "node_processes": [
        "slave",
        "datanode"
    ],
    "name": "PP-Spark-Slave-Node",
    "floating_ip_pool": "fbf94e05-3d97-48c2-83c4-a77a0d2ffea0",
    "flavor_id": "2"
}' | python -m json.tool
```

A sample successful output of the previous API request can be seen as the following:

```
{
    "node_group_template": {
        "auto_security_group": false,
        "availability_zone": null,
        "created_at": "2016-02-20T19:11:06",
        "flavor_id": "2",
        "floating_ip_pool": "fbf94e05-3d97-48c2-83c4-a77a0d2ffea0",
        "hadoop_version": "1.3.1",
        "id": "81940a06-9ff1-42f9-97d9-f9296c015e4d",
        "is_default": false,
        "is_protected": false,
        "is_proxy_gateway": false,
        "is_public": false,
        "name": "PP-Spark-Slave-Node",
        "node_configs": {},
        "node_processes": [
            "slave",
            "datanode"
        ],
        "plugin_name": "spark",
...
```

> To create node group templates using the Sahara API, use the POST method by providing the Tenant ID within the following format:
> `/v1.1/<TENANT_ID>/node-group-templates`

Creating a Spark cluster template

In order to launch the Spark cluster, it might be necessary to collect the template ID for both master and slave node group templates. In our example, the following IDs are collected from the output of the node group template API requests generated previously:

- PP-Spark-Master-Node: f0c833ec-53d5-4a29-8381-8da20c4df707

- PP-Spark-Slave-Node: 81940a06-9ff1-42f9-97d9-f9296c015e4d

For the sake of simplicity, one node per node group will be used to form the Spark cluster template as the following:

```
# curl -g -H 'Content-Type: application/json' \
-H 'X-Auth-Token: bc3243b3177141c3abc684d82db14051' \
-H 'Accept: application/json' \
-X POST cluster-templates \
-d '{
    "plugin_name": "spark",
    "hadoop_version": "1.3.1",
    "node_groups": [
        {
            "name": "PP-Spark-Master-Node",
            "count": 1,
            "node_group_template_id": "f0c833ec-53d5-4a29-8381-
8da20c4df707"
        },
        {
            "name": "PP-Spark-Slave-Node",
            "count": 1,
            "node_group_template_id": "81940a06-9ff1-42f9-97d9-
f9296c015e4d"
        }
    ],
    "name": "PP-Spark-Cluster-Template"
}' | python -m json.tool
```

A successful API request must generate a detailed description of the Spark cluster template showing the template ID and node groups assigned as mentioned in the POST API request. A sample extract of the Curl response can be visualized as the following:

```
{
    "cluster_template": {
        "anti_affinity": [],
        "cluster_configs": {},
        "created_at": "2016-02-20T19:12:53",
        "default_image_id": null,
        "description": null,
```

```
    "hadoop_version": "1.3.1",
    "id": "ba02f228-2e21-4b0b-a4c3-9d3a2a6daa86",
    "is_default": false,
    "is_protected": false,
    "is_public": false,
    "name": "PP-Spark-Cluster-Template",
    "neutron_management_network": null,
    "node_groups": [
...
```

> To create a cluster template using the Sahara API, use the POST
> method by providing the Tenant ID within the following format:
>
> `/v1.1/<TENANT_ID>/cluster-template`

Launching the Spark cluster

Before executing the job, it is necessary to launch the Spark cluster based on the
last cluster template. Keep in mind that it is not possible to run any job before
ensuring the existence of a Spark cluster running in ACTIVE state. Using the Sahara
RESTful API, the Spark cluster can be launched by providing the template cluster
ID generated earlier. Other inputs should be provided to the POST HTTP method
such as the plugin name, the image ID, the name of the cluster, and the management
network ID. In our case, the neutron management network will point to the private
one as the following:

```
# curl -g -H 'Content-Type: application/json' \
-H 'X-Auth-Token: bc3243b3177141c3abc684d82db14051' \
-H 'Accept: application/json' \
-X POST http:// os-cc.packtpub:8386/v1.1/
f4af2ed9ba3c4c079edd02bb7809113d/clusters \
-d '{
    "plugin_name": "spark",
    "hadoop_version": "1.3.1",
    "cluster_template_id": "ba02f228-2e21-4b0b-a4c3-9d3a2a6daa86",
    "default_image_id": "026e348a-d0ac-4e38-9192-436277abba9e",
    "name": "PP-Spark-Cluster",
    "neutron_management_network": "76c28545-4acd-41a7-a41e-93978ad2dd86"
}' | python -m json.tool
```

To query the IDs of the neutron networks in OpenStack, run the following command line in the Network Node (OpenStack Controller Node):

```
# neutron net-list
```

The output of the previous command line might be long. Make sure that it does not return any error regarding the status of the cluster being created:

```
"cluster": {
        "anti_affinity": [],
        "cluster_configs": {
            "HDFS": {
                "dfs.replication": 1
            }
        },
        "cluster_template_id": "ba02f228-2e21-4b0b-a4c3-9d3a2a6daa86",
...
...
"plugin_name": "spark",
        "provision_progress": [],
        "shares": null,
        "status": "Validating",
....
```

The spawning of the cluster might take a few minutes. As shown in the previous output, the cluster status might change from Validating to Spawning. Once completed without errors, the Spark cluster should end up with an Active status. To check the status of the cluster using the Sahara API, run the GET HTTP method command line by providing the cluster ID in the GET command line as follows:

```
# curl -g -H 'Content-Type: application/json' \
-H 'X-Auth-Token: bc3243b3177141c3abc684d82db14051' \
-H 'Accept: application/json' \
-X GET http:// os-cc.packtpub:8386/v1.1/\
f4af2ed9ba3c4c079edd02bb7809113d/clusters/8d543f82-e123-406d-9f3e-
5d25084cd32e | python -m json.tool
```

The last section of the GET HTTP request shows the current provisioning progress of the Spark cluster:

```
...
"provision_progress": [
        {
            "cluster_id": "8d543f82-e123-406d-9f3e-5d25084cd32e",
            "created_at": "2016-02-21T20:51:01",
            "id": "4324f425-78b8-4023-b480-c6dec8e0df52",
            "step_name": "Create Heat stack",
            "step_type": "Engine: create cluster",
            "successful": null,
            "tenant_id": "f4af2ed9ba3c4c079edd02bb7809113d",
            "total": 1,
            "updated_at": null
        }
    ],
    "shares": null,
    "status": "Spawning",
...
```

> To launch a cluster using the Sahara API, use the POST method by providing the Tenant ID within the following format:
>
> `/v1.1/<TENANT_ID>/clusters`

Creating a job binary

The next job binary can be downloaded from the official GitHub Sahara repository found at https://github.com/openstack/sahara/tree/stable/liberty/etc/edp-examples.

We will use the modified version of the WordCount example named the spark-wordcount.jar file. Using the Sahara API, it is possible to create the job binary by pointing the downloaded JAR file mentioned previously as the following:

```
# curl -g -H 'Content-Type: application/json' \
-H 'X-Auth-Token: bc3243b3177141c3abc684d82db14051' \
-H 'Accept: application/json' \
-X PUT http://os-cc.packtpub:8386/v1.1/ f4af2ed9ba3c4c079edd02bb7809113d/
job-binary-internals/spark-wordcount.jar | python -m json.tool
```

The output of the PUT HTTP request looks as follows:

```
{
        "created_at": "2016-02-20T22:10:58",
        "datasize": 28997,
        "id": "7b5f9d88-4042-44b4-8ed3-92db5fe5d9de",
        "is_protected": false,
        "is_public": false,
        "name": "spark-wordcount.jar",
        "tenant_id": "f4af2ed9ba3c4c079edd02bb7809113d",
        "updated_at": null
    },
```

The internal job binary `spark-wordcount.jar` will be stored in the internal database with the ID `7b5f9d88-4042-44b4-8ed3-92db5fe5d9de`.

The next step will demonstrate how to create a job binary using the Sahara API based on the internal ID generated previously. The next command line instructs the Sahara API to create a job binary named `Spark-PP-JB` using the binary object stored in the internal database of Sahara:

```
# curl -g -H 'Content-Type: application/json' \
-H 'X-Auth-Token: bc3243b3177141c3abc684d82db14051' \
-H 'Accept: application/json' \
-X POST http://os-cc.packtpub:8386/v1.1\ /
f4af2ed9ba3c4c079edd02bb7809113d/job-binaries \
-d '{
    "url": "internal-db://7b5f9d88-4042-44b4-8ed3-92db5fe5d9de",
    "name": "Spark-PP-JB",
    "description": "Spark job binary"
}' | python -m json.tool
```

The result of the job binary created can be shown as follows:

```
{
    "job_binary": {
        "created_at": "2016-02-21T23:24:27",
        "description": "Spark job binary",
        "id": "35438059-1c0d-4daa-b005-fdb6b17f3abb",
        "is_protected": false,
        "is_public": false,
```

```
        "name": "Spark-PP-JB",
        "tenant_id": "f4af2ed9ba3c4c079edd02bb7809113d",
        "url": "internal-db://7b5f9d88-4042-44b4-8ed3-92db5fe5d9de"
    }
}
```

 To create a job binary using the Sahara API, use the POST method by providing the Tenant ID and the name of the job binary filename within the following format:

`/v1.1/<TENANT_ID>/job-binary-internals/<NAME-FILE>`

Creating a Spark job template

The next section requires the creation of a job template based on the ID of the job binary created previously. Using the POST method, run the following command line:

```
# curl -g -H 'Content-Type: application/json' \
-H 'X-Auth-Token: bc3243b3177141c3abc684d82db14051' \
-H 'Accept: application/json' \
-X POST http:// os-cc.packtpub:8386/v1.1/
f4af2ed9ba3c4c079edd02bb7809113d/jobs \
-d '{
    "description": "Spark word count job",
    "mains": [
        "acb2b369-b905-4e54-8f12-29391c3c429d"
    ],
    "type": "Spark",
    "name": "Spark-WordCount"
}' | python -m json.tool
```

The next output shows a successful run of the last REST API request:

```
{
    "job": {
        "created_at": "2016-02-22T00:21:24",
        "description": "Spark wordcount job",
        "id": "9475031b-efb2-4f79-b29d-b229311d3a41",
        "interface": [],
        "is_protected": false,
```

```
        "is_public": false,
        "libs": [],
        "mains": [
            {
                "created_at": "2016-02-21T23:24:27",
"description": "Spark job binary",
"id": "35438059-1c0d-4daa-b005-fdb6b17f3abb",
"is_protected": false,
"is_public": false,
"name": "Spark-PP-JB",
"tenant_id": "f4af2ed9ba3c4c079edd02bb7809113d",
"url": "internal-db://7b5f9d88-4042-44b4-8ed3-92db5fe5d9de"
            }
        ],
        "name": "Spark-WordCount",
        "tenant_id": "f4af2ed9ba3c4c079edd02bb7809113d",
        "type": "Spark"
    }
}
```

 To create a job template using the Sahara API, use the POST method by providing the Tenant ID within the following format:
`/v1.1/<TENANT_ID>/jobs`

Executing the Spark job

The last step in our example will instruct the Sahara API to execute the job based on the job template created previously. Additionally, it might be required to figure out how Sahara would find the input text file and where it should save the results once the job is executed. Unlike other jobs types, Spark and Java jobs do not require to specify the data sources as was demonstrated in the first part of this chapter. It is possible to pass such data input and output paths as arguments while configuring the job execution. In order to mimic a real-life scenario, it is possible to use the same Swift container created in the first part of this chapter and upload a new object text file called countme with the following content:

```
OpenStack
Sahara
OpenStack
```

```
Sahara
Sahara
OpenStack
OpenStack
Sahara
Sahara
Sahara
Sahara
```

In this example, results can be collected from HDFS. The RESTful API command line will be as follows:

```
# curl -g -H 'Content-Type: application/json' \
-H 'X-Auth-Token: bc3243b3177141c3abc684d82db14051' \
-H 'Accept: application/json' \
-X POST http://os-cc.packtpub:8386/v1.1/\
f4af2ed9ba3c4c079edd02bb7809113d/jobs/9475031b-efb2-4f79-b29d-
b229311d3a41/execute \
-d '{
    "cluster_id": "fb2a4f7f-8d09-4916-a1d5-caae400989be",
    "job_configs": {
        "configs": {
            "fs.swift.service.sahara.username": "admin",
            "fs.swift.service.sahara.password": "bigpassword",
            "edp.java.main_class": "sahara.edp.spark.SparkWordCount",
            "edp.spark.adapt_for_swift": true
        },
        "args": ["swift://input.sahara/countme", "hdfs://os-cc.
packtpub:8386/tmp/spark-edp/results"]
    }
}' | python -m json.tool
```

The parameters highlighted in bold describe the workflow of the execution of the Spark job. If the edp.spark.adapt_for_swift option is not set explicitly to true, Swift paths will not be accessed, although the username and password are provided. Args will instruct the job to look for input from the Swift container and drop any result to the internal node running HDFS.

A typical output of the job execution POST request shows a PENDING status at the first glance. The status is triggered once the job injects its configuration instruction to the running cluster created previously:

```
"job_execution": {
        "cluster_id": "fb2a4f7f-8d09-4916-a1d5-caae400989be",
        "created_at": "2016-02-22T00:48:52",
        "id": "5bf6b908-d4d8-4d56-8585-0521c920e925",
        "info": {
            "status": "PENDING"
        },
...
...
```

To check output results, log in to the Spark master node and navigate to the output path file `results`. The output contains all words and the number of times that they occur as follows:

```
(OpenStack, 4)
(Sahara, 7)
```

Extending the Spark job

The continuous increase of the fleet of servers running a specific application is a great indicator of the success of the software product. Thousands of users are initiating tremendous traffic that keeps increasing every day. On the other hand, development and quality assurance departments will always need an easy way to debug and profile their applications, tune their hardware performance, and increase the application security level. This can be achieved by keeping an eye on log files on a daily basis. Web and application servers are the most common servers that generate a huge number and big log files. Depending on how developers and operators have configured their servers, logging access, error, and any other customized log information is essential. This will help with understanding how their application is behaving, and most importantly, how users were managing to access the right functionality of their product. Storing and analyzing an immense number with a large size of log files is challenging. Essentially, a real use case is to analyze log files in real time. Using Spark on Sahara for this purpose can be very simple and efficient. The previous example demonstrates a simple use case when one aims to run a counter job on a simple file. However, extending the job to run over terabytes of unstructured data stored in HDFS will raise a new challenge: how to scale the Spark cluster to keep moving with the same performance. More customized jobs require preparation on how to scale the Spark cluster on the fly.

Traditionally, this can be achieved by installing a similar node from scratch, configure its network connectivity, and join the cluster. That might take a long time and can be an error-prone process. With Sahara, such a workflow looks different; what you need is just to push a button and you are ready to go. In the previous example, a Spark cluster was provisioned with only one Master and one Slave node. When it comes to face and analyze more data and run a customized elastic job processing, we will need more nodes. More specifically, we will need additional Spark Slave nodes on the fly. The greatest thing about Sahara is its simplicity. The following illustration demonstrates how Sahara is able to scale the existing Spark cluster while keeping the job running and analyzing new log and large files stored in HDFS. From the cluster tab, press the `Scale` button:

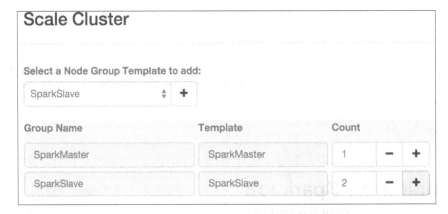

It is possible to increase the number of Spark Slave nodes in the count column. In our example, we will add a new Spark Slave and verify our new setup. By confirming the scale operation in the Scale Cluster dashboard, Sahara will add a new instance and bring the Spark Cluster active within the new cluster setup as follows:

This can also be verified from the dashboard as well as the `sahara-engine.log` file as follows:

```
72-b390809dc6ff] Cluster status has been changed. New status=Scaling: Spawning
2016-03-27 23:55:24.429 26281 INFO sahara.utils.cluster [req-95fa28be-0d46-4b1
72-b390809dc6ff] Cluster status has been changed. New status=Adding Instances
```

The next Sahara stage will start the Hadoop services on the new node and update its host file. In this way, the new Spark Slave is able to join the cluster and boost the elastic job processing to go beyond its original limits.

```
c5db15, cluster: 7741f4d0-723c-4302-a872-b390809dc6ff] NTP successfully configured
2016-03-27 22:13:33.093 26281 INFO sahara.utils.cluster [req-74a2d18a-3a50-457e-8c8
72-b390809dc6ff] Cluster status has been changed. New status=Starting
2016-03-27 22:16:07.707 26281 INFO sahara.plugins.spark.plugin [req-74a2d18a-3a50-4
4302-a872-b390809dc6ff] Hadoop services have been started
```

Scaling the Spark cluster is also done by removing a node when it is needed. This holds true when data analyzed decreases and Spark instances become mostly ideal. Using the same Scale window, removing a Spark Slave from the Slave can be achieved by subtracting one node from the Count column. Sahara will start decommissioning the cluster as shown in the trunked `sahara-engine` log file:

```
New status=Decommissioning
00:14.896 1368 INFO sahara.utils.cluster
New status=Scaling
```

Deleting the instance will not affect the processed job in the existing Spark Sahara when it come back to the Active State:

```
Spark service has been started
26281 INFO sahara.plugins.spark.plugin
Cluster has been started successfully
```

Summary

In this chapter, we looked at executing jobs in Sahara by examining the running job workflow on top of OpenStack. The EDP project in OpenStack with the last releases becomes a great flavor to run complex jobs on a Hadoop cluster in no time with the support of many other plugins that have been cited in this chapter.

This chapter also covered how to launch a Spark cluster and execute a simple job using the Sahara REST API. By the end of the chapter, an example of a real-world scenario was discussed and it was explained how Sahara can simplify the scalability challenge. Running more complex jobs within tons of unstructured data will undoubtedly need a simple and easy approach to tackle future data growth issues. The chapter has demonstrated how Sahara is capable of accomplishing such a necessity.

The next chapter will go in depth on more advanced options that Sahara offers for a more sophisticated data processing environment.

5
Discovering Advanced Features with Sahara

As the Hadoop infrastructure starts to grow, several new requirements will start to appear such as automating the creation of images, keeping the Hadoop cluster resilient to failure, and looking to the best outfit for the big data cluster networking configuration. In this chapter, we will discuss several topics that come up with Sahara, which offers in the latest stable releases more advanced functionalities that allow setting up a more customized Hadoop cluster within more possibilities and choices of configuration. This chapter will examine the following topics:

- Discussing different plugins supported by Sahara in the current version
- Creating images for different Sahara plugins using image tools out of the box
- Checking the requirements and limitations for each plugin in Sahara
- Learning what is an affinity group and how to use it in Sahara
- Understanding data locality and how to use it in Sahara
- Discussing different networking configurations in Sahara in the current setup
- Outlining the use case of block storage in Sahara and how to maximize data performance within the Hadoop cluster on top of OpenStack

Sahara plugins

Sahara exposes several provisioning plugins in order to deploy a specific data processing distribution. This becomes highly important for vendor plugins wishing to write code that comply with their API and distribution. The OpenStack Liberty release supports the following provisioning plugins as shown in Horizon:

Data Processing Plugins

Title	Supported Versions
Vanilla Apache Hadoop	2.6.0 2.7.1
Hortonworks Data Platform	2.0.6
Apache Spark	1.3.1 1.0.0
Cloudera Plugin	5 5.3.0 5.4.0

Provisioning plugins sit in the middle of the architecture of Sahara as shown as follows:

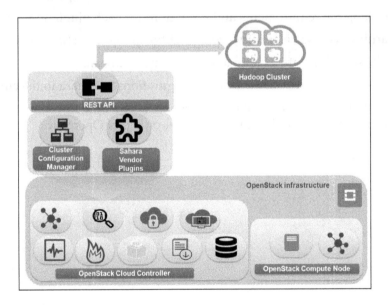

Each OpenStack release provides a new version of a plugin. Thus, in order to support an existing Hadoop framework or to leverage a specific version of the Hadoop API, it might be essential to select the right version and check the supported features and updates for each plugin. To make it much easier, the next section will highlight different supported plugins and versions in the Liberty release by examining the capabilities of each of them.

Vanilla Apache Hadoop

The Vanilla Apache Hadoop plugin in the Liberty release supports the Hadoop 2.6.0 and 2.7.1 versions. OpenStack also supports Hadoop 1.x.x versions in previous releases (Icehouse and Juno). The Apache Hadoop plugin starts to grab tarballs from Apache to install the Hadoop cluster during the spawning status of the Hadoop instances creation phase. Basically, the Apache Vanilla plugin expects to find Hadoop already pulled and installed in the image that will be later uploaded and registered in Glance. Thus, preparing the right image for Vanilla Apache is required in order to run properly an Apache Hadoop cluster. In *Chapter 3*, *Using OpenStack Sahara*, we have downloaded a pre-built image and tagged it in Sahara Image Registry. In this section, we will start building an image for the Apache Vanilla plugin.

Building an image for the Apache Vanilla plugin

In this section, a few instructions will guide you to build a CentOS image with Apache Hadoop version 2.x.x. To do so, a very helpful tool, Disk Image Builder, can be used.

> Disk Image Builder is a set of components and tools allowing you to build a customized number of disk and ramdisk images for OpenStack. The images are referenced using elements that designate the image built. An element is generally a set of code that describes the image composition. Disk Image Builder can be found at GitHub: `https://github.com/openstack/diskimage-builder`

1. Create a new directory where the Disk Image Builder and Sahara image elements will reside:

   ```
   # mkdir images
   ```

   ```
   # cd images
   ```

   ```
   # git clone https://github.com/openstack/sahara-image-elements
   ```

> For more information, please check the following URL:
> `https://github.com/openstack/sahara-image-`
> `elements`

2. Run the `tox` command line to build images. It will install all the required Python packages and executes `diskimage-create.sh`. The script will download and populate the necessary parameters for disk images environment variables for different operating systems including Ubuntu, Fedora, and CentOS. If `tox` is not installed, run the following command line:

```
# pip install tox
```

The next command line will create a CentOS 7 image within Vanilla Hadoop version 2.7.1:

```
# tox -e venv -- sahara-image-create -u -p vanilla -v 2 -i centos7
```

> The `tox` command line within the Sahara image building elements has the following syntax:
>
> ```
> # tox -e env -- sahara-image-create -u \
> -p SAHARA_PLUGIN \
> -v HADOOP_VERSION_TARGET \
> -i OPERATION_SYSTEM_TARGET
> ```
>
> Where:
>
> `SAHARA_PLUGIN`: Defines the Sahara plugin that will be used
>
> `HADOOP_VERSION_TARGET`: Defines which version of Hadoop within the provisioning plugin version will be used
>
> `OPERATION_SYSTEM_TARGET`: Defines the base operating system including Ubuntu, Fedora, CentOS 6.x, and CentOS 7

The `-u` flag might be required to instruct the disk builder script to install any missing packages for a complete image building process.

For the preceding command output, `tox` will start building the image using the image elements as follows:

```
...

Building elements: base  centos7 vm sahara-version ntp xfs-tools hadoop
oozie mysql disable-firewall hive openjdk

...
```

The command could take a while before finishing downloading the image, the Hadoop distribution, and installing it in the correspondent image:

```
Installing GRUB2...
--------------------- PROFILING ----------------------

Target: finalise.d

Script                                    Seconds
-------------------------------------     ---------

01-clean-old-kernels                      11.882
11-selinux-fixfiles-restore               13.529
50-remove-bogus-udev-links                0.007
51-bootloader                             1.505
99-cleanup-tmp-grub                       0.007

------------------- END PROFILING --------------------
'/tmp/image.434uqKyA/mnt//etc/dib-manifests' -> 'centos7_sahara_vanilla_hadoop_2_7_1_latest.d/dib-manifests'
'/tmp/image.434uqKyA/mnt//etc/dib-manifests/dib_environment' -> 'centos7_sahara_vanilla_hadoop_2_7_1_latest.
'/tmp/image.434uqKyA/mnt//etc/dib-manifests/dib_arguments' -> 'centos7_sahara_vanilla_hadoop_2_7_1_latest.d/
DIB_YUM_REPO_CONF is not set - no repo configurations will be cleaned up
--------------------- PROFILING ----------------------

Target: cleanup.d

Script                                    Seconds
-------------------------------------     ---------

00-clean-java-vars                        0.004
01-ccache                                 0.017
01-copy-manifests-dir                     0.069
51-bootloader                             0.026
99-remove-yum-repo-conf                   0.004
99-tidy-logs                              0.061

------------------- END PROFILING --------------------
/dev/loop2: [0041]:10903100 (/tmp/image.VOfE6bbN/image.raw)
Converting image using qemu-img convert
Image file centos7_sahara_vanilla_hadoop_2_7_1_latest.qcow2 created...
_____ summary _____
  venv: commands succeeded
  congratulations :)
```

The new CentOS 7 Hadoop image is generated with the qcow2 format as shown in the following illustration:

```
   26 Dec   7 01:25 centos7_sahara_vanilla_hadoop_2_7_1_latest.d
  1.3G Dec   7 01:27 centos7_sahara_vanilla_hadoop_2_7_1_latest.qcow2
```

 Using a different hypervisor in OpenStack requires converting the previous generated image to the appropriate format using the qemu-img utility.

Vanilla Apache requirements and limitations

Within the OpenStack Liberty release, several changes and updates have been used to support Hadoop version 2.x.x. Creating a Hadoop cluster using the Vanilla plugin should take into consideration which node process will be included as mandatory. The spaces following the matrix highlights a few requirements and limitations when using Vanilla Hadoop version 2.x.x in the OpenStack Liberty release per cluster:

Process name	Status	Number	Node dependency
NameNode	Mandatory	Exactly 1	-
ResourceManager	Optional	At most 1	-
SecondaryNode	Optional	At most 1	-
HistoryServer	Optional	At most 1	-
Oozie	Optional	At most 1	ResourceManager HistoryServer
NodeManager	Optional	1 or more	ResourceManager
HiveServer	Optional	At most 1	-
DataNode	Optional	1 or more	-

It might be imperative to satisfy certain conditions to lead to a successful Elastic Data Processing task using the Vanilla plugin. This will require picking up Oozie and Hive to the nodes templates from the process list.

Hortonworks Data Platform plugin

The **Hortonworks Data Platform (HDP)** plugin in Sahara enables the creation and management of a HDP cluster on top of OpenStack. The nirvana of HDP comes from the usage of Apache Ambari that facilitates the provisioning of a HDP cluster on OpenStack.

Apache Ambari is the first open source project that provides a framework for provisioning, managing, and monitoring an Apache Hadoop stack. To read more about Apache Ambari, follow this link: http://ambari. apache.org/

Building an image for the HDP plugin

Compared with the Apache Vanilla plugin, the Hortonworks plugin operates in two different ways:

- Using a minimal version installation of an image within only an operating system within an enabled cloud-init. This will require a complete download and installation phase of all necessary packages during cluster provisioning.

- Using preinstalled HDP images.

> There are some caveats to using a minimal image installation that must be considered when provisioning many nodes in large clusters. This can take a longer time and could jeopardize network performance connectivity since all the nodes will require several packages to be downloaded.

For faster cluster provisioning, it might be more convenient to prepare pre-populated images using Disk Image Builder as shown in the previous section. Since the sahara-image-elements tool is already downloaded, it is possible to build an HDP image based on CentOS and supporting the 2.0.6 version:

```
# tox -e venv -- sahara-image-create -p hdp -v 2 -i centos
```

> HDP supports only CentOS 5.X and CentOS 6.X. It also supports RHEL 5.X and later. Note that CentOS 7 is not supported yet at the time of writing this book.

The script will download and install accordingly the needed JDK packages dependency, the Hortonworks Data Platform 2.0.6 distribution, and Apache Ambari.

HDP requirements and limitations

Although the current HDP plugin supports only CentOS Linux distribution for the cluster guests' operating systems, the HDP plugin is very overwhelming in terms of Hadoop cluster node processes. The creation of a Hadoop cluster from Horizon requires at least the existence of the following node processes in the cluster:

Process name	Status	Number	Node dependency
NameNode	Mandatory	Exactly 1	YARN
Ambari Server	Mandatory	At most 1	NameNode
ResourceManager	Mandatory	At most 1	-
YARN_CLIENT	Mandatory	At most 1	-

Process name	Status	Number	Node dependency
DataNode	Optional	1 or more	-
NodeManager	Optional	1 or more	-
MAPREDUCE2_ CLIENT	Optional	At most 1	-

The next table summarizes the node processes requirements that have to exist in a HDP cluster within the HA HDFS enabled feature:

Process name	Status	Number	Node dependency
NameNode	Mandatory	at least 2	YARN
JOURNALNODE	Mandatory	At least 3	(2) NameNodes
ZOOKEEPER_ SERVER	Mandatory	At least 3	(2) NameNodes
YARN_CLIENT	Mandatory	At most 1	-

 The number of JOURNALNODE processes in the HDP HA cluster should be an odd-count number.

Cloudera Distribution Hadoop plugin

Cloudera Distribution Hadoop (CDH) is an open source Apache Hadoop distribution that aims to perform a complete big data workflow under the Hadoop environment. Cloudera provides a Cloudera Manager core component, which allows you to manage a scalable distributed data processing platform of large datasets. Cloudera Manager enables an automated way of installing and configuring CDH clusters. Eventually, Sahara provides a stable CDH plugin that allows deploying a CDH stack completely managed and centrally operated by Cloudera Manager. Nothing will be installed manually; we let Sahara do that for us.

As shown in the next illustration, by specifying the cluster template, different virtual machines in the cluster will be created and provisioned by Heat. A CDH cluster requires the existence of Cloudera Manager in the master node. Once the cluster has been created, Cloudera Manager will be available on the master node that can be accessible by means of the Cloudera Manager API provided by the CDH plugin. This is essential in order to provision other services in the cluster.

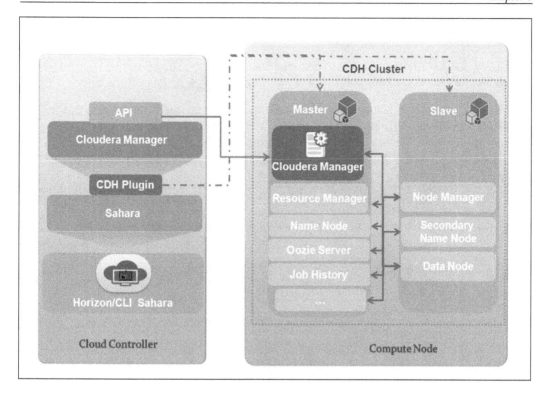

Building an image for the CDH plugin

In this section, we will build an image based on CentOS using the Disk Image Builder tool. In the same Sahara image elements directory, issue the tox command line. In this example, we will create a CentOS image supporting Cloudera version 5.4:

```
# tox -e venv -- sahara-image-create -p cloudera -v 5.4 -i centos
```

 The Sahara Cloudera plugin supports only Ubuntu and CentOS images.

Building the image can take a long time. The base image will be downloaded, and start pre-installing all the required packages for the CDH package including Cloudera Manager into the image.

To start using the image in Sahara, be sure to upload the image in Glance and register it afterwards into Sahara.

```
# glance image-create --name  CDH-CentOS  --disk-format=qcow2
--container=bare < ./centos_sahara_cdh_hadoop_5_4_1_latest.qcow2
```

As shown in *Chapter 3, Using OpenStack Sahara*, the image has to be tagged in the Sahara tab in Horizon. It is possible to use the Sahara command-line interface to register the image. The next subsequent command lines will register the image in Sahara and tag it as 5.4.0. First, export the image ID in your shell environment as the following:

```
# glance image-list --name CDH-CentOS
```

```
+--------------------+------------------------------------------+
| Property           | Value                                    |
+--------------------+------------------------------------------+
| checksum           | 301d56b85f90c78c1d68c96fa24c6d07         |
| container_format   | bare                                     |
| created_at         | 2015-12-13T20:38:24Z                     |
| disk_format        | qcow2                                    |
| id                 | 68daa0f1-c4df-4637-8d4a-7d5c47fd4d21     |
| min_disk           | 0                                        |
| min_ram            | 0                                        |
| name               | CDH-CentOS                               |
| owner              | 81d75084bb3b46b683d4d3313ced9c13         |
| protected          | False                                    |
| size               | 3264479232                               |
| status             | active                                   |
| tags               | []                                       |
| updated_at         | 2015-12-13T20:38:55Z                     |
| virtual_size       | None                                     |
| visibility         | private                                  |
+--------------------+------------------------------------------+
```

```
# export IMG_ID="68daa0f1-c4df-4637-8d4a-7d5c47fd4d21"
```

```
# sahara image-register --id $IMG_ID --username cloud-user
```

```
# sahara image-register --id $IMG_ID --tag cdh
```

```
# sahara image-register --id $IMG_ID --tag 5.4.0
```

To check the status of the CDH image in Sahara, enter the following command line:

```
# sahara image-list
```

```
+------------+--------------------------------------+------------+------------+-------------+
| name       | id                                   | username   | tags       | description |
+------------+--------------------------------------+------------+------------+-------------+
| CDH-CentOS | 68daa0f1-c4df-4637-8d4a-7d5c47fd4d21 | cloud-user | 5.4.0, cdh | None        |
+------------+--------------------------------------+------------+------------+-------------+
```

CDH requirements and limitations

In order to validate a well-operating CDH cluster in Sahara, it is necessary to take into consideration a few requirements summarized in the following table:

Process name	Status	Number	Node dependency
NodeManager	Mandatory	Exactly 1	-
NameNode	Mandatory	Exactly 1	-
SecondartyNameNode	Mandatory	Exactly 1	-
ResourceManager	Optional	At most 1	JobHistory
DataNode	Mandatory	1 or more	dfs_replication enabled
NodeManager	Optional	1 or more	ResourceManager
JobHistory	Optional	At most 1	-
Oozie	Optional	At most 1	DataNode NodeManager JobHistory
Hive	Optional	At most 1	HiveServer, ResourceManager
Hue Server	Optional	At most 1	Hive Oozie
HistoryServer	Optional	At most 1	ResourceManager
HBASE_MASTER	Optional	At most 1	Zookeeper HBASE_REGIONSERVER
HBASE_REGIONSERVER	Optional	At most 1	HBASE_MASTER
FLUME	Optional	At most 1	DATANODE
SENTRYSERVER	Optional	At most 1	ZooKeeper DataNode
SQOOPSERVER	Optional	At most 1	DataNode NodeManager JobHistory
SOLR_SERVER	Optional	At most 1	ZooKeeper DataNode
HBASE_INDEXER	Optional	At most 1	DataNode ZooKeeper SolrServer HBASE_MASTER

Process name	Status	Number	Node dependency
IMPALA_CATALOG_SERVER	Optional	At most 1	DataNode
			Impala_Metastore
			Impala_StatesStore
IMPALA_StatesStore	Optional	1 or more	(Installed per DataNode)

Apache Spark plugin

At the time of writing this book, the Spark plugin allows you to provision Apache Spark clusters on OpenStack in standalone mode. The plugin does not yet support either YARN or Mesos.

It is possible to take advantage of the usage of Mesos or YARN in a traditional standalone cluster deployment. This allows sharing a cluster of nodes between several frameworks.

For example, by supporting Mesos in the Spark cluster, the Spark master instance can be replaced by a Mesos master and be the cluster manager.

 To read more about Mesos, refer to the official website of the Mesos project: `http://mesos.apache.org/`

Building an image for the Spark plugin

Sahara-image-elements can be used to prepare an image for cluster provisioning based on Apache Spark. Like the CDH plugin, images generated contain the required packages installed and configured to run the Hadoop cluster. Spark will be installed automatically when creating the image. On the other hand, it is possible to create only Ubuntu images.

That makes the creation of the image straightforward as the following:

```
# tox -e venv -- sahara-image-create -p spark -v 1.3.1
```

The base image will be downloaded, and start pre-installing all the required packages for the Spark package.

To start using the image in Sahara, be sure to upload the image in Glance and register it afterwards into Sahara.

```
# glance image-create --name  Spark  --disk-format=qcow2 --container=bare
< ./ubuntu_sahara_spark_hadoop_1_3_1_latest.qcow2
```

In order to use the generated image in Sahara, the image has to be tagged in Horizon possibly with Spark and 1.3.1 tags. It might be possible to use the Sahara command-line interface to register the image. The next subsequent command lines will register the image in Sahara and tag it as 1.3.1. First, export the image ID in your shell environment as the following:

```
# glance image-list --name Spark
```

```
| disk format   | qcow2                                  |
| id            | 7a776591-e6a6-4303-b292-4c529363b4f3   |
| min_disk      | 0                                      |
| min_ram       | 0                                      |
| name          | Spark                                  |
```

```
# export IMG_ID="7a776591-e6a6-4303-b292-4c529363b4f3"
# sahara image-register --id $IMG_ID --username cloud-user
# sahara image-register --id $IMG_ID --tag spark
# sahara image-register --id $IMG_ID --tag 1.3.1
```

To check the status of the Spark image in Sahara, enter the following command line:

```
# sahara image-show --name Spark
```

```
+-----------------------+------------------------------------------+
| Property              | Value                                    |
+-----------------------+------------------------------------------+
| _sahara_tag_1.3.1     | True                                     |
| _sahara_tag_spark     | True                                     |
| _sahara_username      | cloud-user                               |
| checksum              | 19640faead38e82528af6d85cd9894c5         |
| container_format      | bare                                     |
| created_at            | 2015-12-04T23:30:01Z                     |
| disk_format           | qcow2                                    |
| id                    | 7a776591-e6a6-4303-b292-4c529363b4f3     |
| min_disk              | 0                                        |
| min_ram               | 0                                        |
| name                  | Spark                                    |
| owner                 | cf3349904cc54dd488efaa24b872b0b7         |
| protected             | False                                    |
| size                  | 957378048                                |
| status                | active                                   |
| tags                  | []                                       |
| updated_at            | 2015-12-04T23:33:56Z                     |
| virtual_size          | None                                     |
| visibility            | public                                   |
+-----------------------+------------------------------------------+
```

Spark requirements and limitations

The Spark plugin in Sahara is considered very simple to deploy an Apache Spark cluster. The processes currently supported are only for HDFS DataNode, HDFS NameNode, Master, and Slave.

The cluster topology for Spark cluster deployment in Sahara can be outlined as the following:

Process name	Status	Number	Node dependency
HDFS NameNode	Mandatory	Exactly 1	ALL
HDFS DataNode	Mandatory	At least 1	ALL
Master	Mandatory	Exactly 1	ALL
Slave	Mandatory	At least 1	ALL

Affinity and anti-affinity

The term **affinity** deals essentially with the way of grouping and specifying in which host or hypervisor a virtual machine should run. In OpenStack, it is possible to add an instance to a particular affinity group while creating it. This will instruct Nova to launch the instance in a particular host depending on the affinity policy.

The OpenStack Compute service or Nova determines how to dispatch a compute resource request by means of nova-scheduler. This is an internal Compute OpenStack service allowing on which host a VM will be launched based on certain algorithms and strategies called filters. In the context of affinity, the nova scheduler can use several affinity policies and algorithms such as ServerGroupAntiAffinityFilter, ServerGroupAffinityFilter. For more information on scheduling in OpenStack, check the following:

OpenStack official community: http://docs.openstack.org/liberty/config-reference/content/section_compute-scheduler.html

Affinity policies can be classified as the following:

- Affinity (affinity enabled): Instructs the OpenStack Compute service to launch the selected instances in the same host (hypervisor machine)

- Anti-affinity (affinity disabled): Instructs the OpenStack Compute service to launch the selected instances in different hosts (hypervisor machine)

The next illustration shows an example on how nova-scheduler can dispatch instances in different compute hosts using affinity and anti-affinity groups:

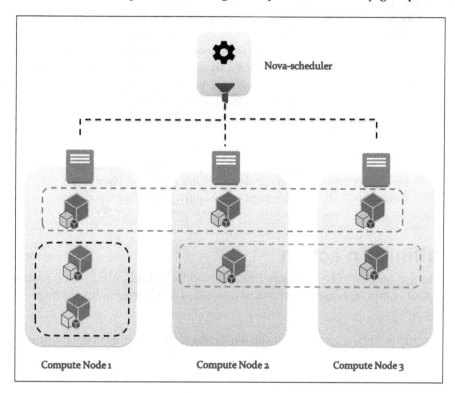

As shown in the previous diagram, the dotted black grouping square presents one affinity group in which instances belong to the same host, **Compute Node 1**. The blue and red groups each present an anti-affinity group in which instances are hosted in different hosts; no instances of the same anti-affinity group will be spawned in the same physical host.

In OpenStack, it is possible to use the nova command line to create a first server group with a certain policy. For example, the next command line will create a new server group called `pp_anti_aff` within the anti-affinity policy:

```
# nova server-group-create pp_anti_aff
```

This will instruct Nova that a new server group has been created and is ready to include more instances as members of the group. In Sahara, the anti-affinity feature is very useful in order to ensure a high available cluster. Although a CDH cluster is running in HA mode, it will not make sense if both Cloudera Manager, for example, are being spawned and running in the same hypervisor. In case of machine failure, it loses the entire cluster. Anti-affinity can be enabled and specified in Sahara in each cluster template setup for every plugin. By selecting a service node process to run in anti-affinity mode, Sahara instructs nova in which machine a Hadoop instance will run. Basically, it is not necessary to create a server group manually; Sahara will create automatically a new server group per cluster in which Hadoop instances can be members of the anti-affinity group.

 To use this feature, make sure to have more than one compute node in the OpenStack environment setup. If only one hypervisor exists, Sahara might throw an error message while spawning a Hadoop cluster.

Anti-affinity in action

In order to use anti-affinity functionality exposed by Sahara, it might be required to add a new compute node in our setup described in *Chapter 2, Integrating OpenStack Sahara*.

The new setup will be expanded as shown in the following topology diagram:

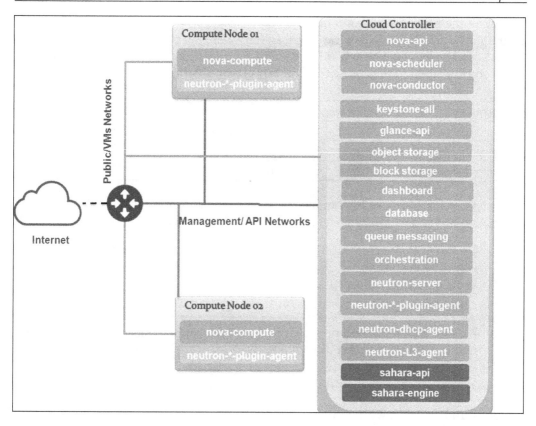

Adding a new compute node can be accomplished in different ways:

- Install a new machine in VirtualBox and assign the same number of virtual network interfaces, the same types of network adapters, and the same IP pool addresses. Then install nova packages and configure manually the compute service.

- Make a snapshot of the existing compute node. Create a new virtual machine in VirtualBox based on the created snapshot using the Clone option. Change the IP addressing and configuration (check MAC address conflict) in the cloned virtual machine, and reconfigure and rerun the Nova service to point to its current IP.

- Create a new virtual machine with a fresh operating system. Assign the same number of network interfaces to the same networks where Compute Node 01 is connected. Rerun Packstack in the controller to install and join the new compute node to the OpenStack environment.

Adopting the first or the second method can be error-prone if it is not carefully reconfigured. Using Packstack can be straightforward by performing a few changes in the answer file. The next wizard table cites the network setup interfaces for the new compute node in the current VirtualBox environment:

Hostname	Interface	Adapter type	IP Address
Compute Node 02	eth0	Host-only	10.10.10.49/24
Compute Node 02	eth1	Host-only	10.20.10.49/24
Compute Node 02	eth2	NAT	DHCP

The next wizard describes how to use Packstack to join automatically the new compute node to the OpenStack cluster:

1. On the new cloud controller node, edit the value of CONFIG_NOVA_COMPUTE_ HOSTS by adding the IP address of the new compute node in the answers_pp.txt file as the following:

   CONFIG_NOVA_COMPUTE_HOSTS=10.10.10.48, 10.10.10.49

2. No major changes will be performed on the current compute and controller nodes. Adding the next directive to the answer file will not affect any running configuration during the Packstack run:

   EXCLUDE_SERVERS=10.10.10.47,10.10.10.48

3. Run Packstack with new configurations to join the new compute node to the OpenStack cluster:

   # packstack --answer-file=answers_pp.txt

Packstack will run by installing the new hypervisor. This can be checked when it finishes without error by running the next command line on the cloud controller:

 # nova service-list

Now with an additional hypervisor installed in the OpenStack virtual environment, it might be possible to make use of the anti-affinity functionality provided by Sahara.

The next example will create a new Spark cluster using Sahara. Anti-affinity can be enabled within one or more of the following Spark processes: **master**, **slave**, **namenode**, **datanode**.

1. Create a first master node group template:

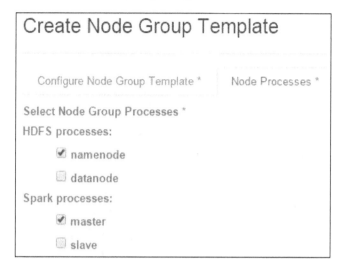

2. Create a second slave node group template:

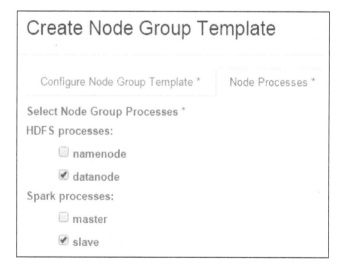

3. Create a cluster template with **datanode** anti-affinity enabled as the following:

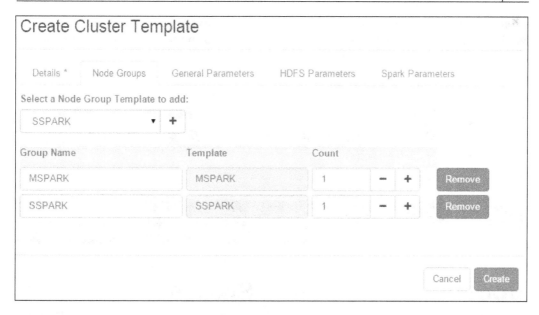

Doing so will make sure that both nodes will not be spawned in the same compute node. Each compute node will spawn one Spark instance but not both. This is because the DataNode process is expected to run on both machines, the anti-affinity lists that such a process can be associated with an instance running in a different hypervisor rather than the same one.

Once the cluster is spawned and running, it might be interesting to check in which host each Spark instance is running. To do so, pick up the name of both nodes via the next command line on the cloud controller as the following:

```
# nova list
```

Identifying where each instance is running in which hypervisor can be accomplished via the following command lines where cn01 refers to the first compute node and cn02 refers to the second compute node:

```
# nova hypervisor-servers cn01
```

```
+--------------------------------------+---------------------+---------------+---------------------+
| ID                                   | Name                | Hypervisor ID | Hypervisor Hostname |
+--------------------------------------+---------------------+---------------+---------------------+
| 5885d359-96d1-4072-97fc-59c8c178fc6f | instance-0000005d   | 1             | cn01                |
```

```
# nova hypervisor-servers   cn02
```

```
+--------------------------------------+---------------------+---------------+---------------------+
| ID                                   | Name                | Hypervisor ID | Hypervisor Hostname |
+--------------------------------------+---------------------+---------------+---------------------+
| e4a6188d-9e56-4d4c-8add-26f59ed97871 | instance-0000005e   | 2             | cn02                |
```

Boosting Elastic Data Processing performance

Processing data in Hadoop can be very expensive in terms of network latency cost. In a Hadoop cluster, all data is being distributed to all nodes residing in the cluster. Ideally, HDFS splits the data file into chunks to be analyzed by several nodes. Additionally, each chunk of data will be replicated across different machines for data loss resiliency. Basically, every chunk of data is treated in Hadoop as a record broken into a specific format depending on the application logic.

When it comes to processing an assigned record set of data by each node, the Hadoop framework maps each process to the location of data based on the knowledge for the HDFS. To avoid any unneeded network transfers, processes start reading the data located from the local disk for best computation results.

Eventually, this strategy is very cost-effective, which considers that moving computation is performance-wise than moving data. The technique of data-locality in Hadoop makes the data process-aware, which enables for example the task tracker nodes to run jobs locally for their input stream.

The data locality concept depends essentially on the following key points:

- Nodes topology for proper task assignment
- Distance between nodes
- Task scheduling
- Closest data nodes within the fetched data under question

To make use of such a great technique in Sahara, it is important to outline in a nutshell how the traditional topology is being presented in a Hadoop cluster:

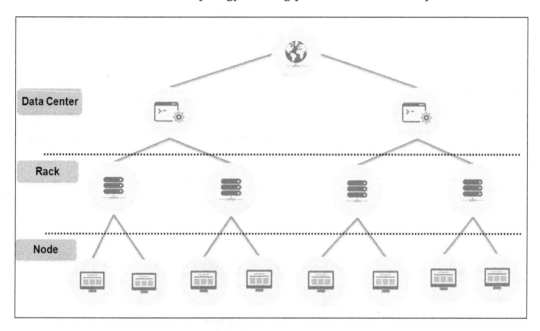

The previous diagram takes into account three different network layers: **Data Center**, **Rack**, and **Hadoop Node**. This design will instruct, for example, the task tracker and data node to be spawned on the same rack. However, the previous topology does not take into account the host/hypervisor layer in order to map more specifically where to execute tasks, for example. Task tracker can be executed in different nodes across the network in the Hadoop cluster. However, other nodes existing in the same hypervisor can also communicate to achieve the same process request that is not known in the first glance.

To work around this limitation, the new Hadoop network layer topology introduces a fourth layer as illustrated in the next diagram:

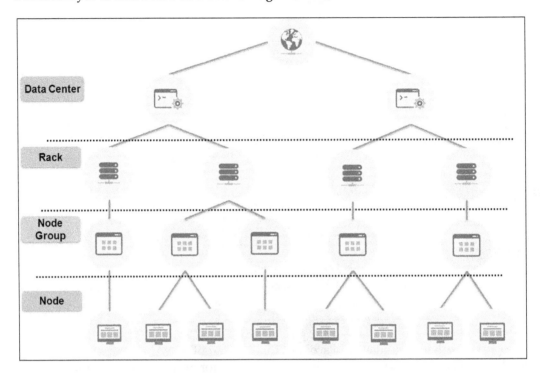

The new **Node Group** layer pinpoints the machine hosting the virtual machines. Nodes residing in the same hypervisor machine will be able to be mapped and communicate between each other, which reduces network overhead.

Sahara has been developed to support three and four-layer network topology as has been highlighted previously. It uses the compute host ID to identify which Hadoop node group cluster will be used. Sahara can be configured in order to take advantage of such a great technique as the following:

1. Enable the data locality feature in the Sahara configuration file /etc/ sahara/sahara.conf as follows:

```
[DEFAULT]
enable_data_locality=True
```

2. The next step may require enabling the support of the four-layer Hadoop topology. This can be done by adding the following content to the Sahara configuration file:

```
enable_hypervisor_awareness = True
```

3. In order to comply with the same topology layer described previously, Sahara requires a full description of the hypervisor topology, which can be specified a topology file called `hypervisor.topology`. This can be described in the Sahara configuration file as the following:

```
[DEFAULT]
compute_topology_file=/etc/sahara/hypervisor.topology
```

4. The `hypervisor.toplogy` file contains simply a brief mapping of which hypervisor or compute node to which rack. To get the right compute nodes as configured in the OpenStack cluster, type the following command:

```
# nova list
```

5. The next file maps `cn01.pp` first compute node to the first rack and `cn02.pp` as a second compute node to the second rack in the OpenStack environment.

```
# nano /etc/sahara/hypervisor.topology

cn01.pp /rack01

cn02.pp /rack02
```

6. When using data locality for Swift input streams in Hadoop, Sahara might require the definition of a swift topology description. This will be defined in a new topology file in the Sahara configuration file called `object_storage.topology` as the following:

```
[DEFAULT]
...
swift_topology_file=/etc/sahara/object_storage.topology
```

7. Since we have installed the Swift node on the cloud controller, the topology file can have only one line pointing to the cloud controller on `rack01` as the following:

```
# nano /etc/sahara/hypervisor.topology
cc01.pp /rack01
```

Defining the network

Apparently, one of the most pertinent questions that pops up when designing an OpenStack environment is the network setup and configuration. Networking in OpenStack might appear complex when we consider using Neutron instead of the Nova-network service. Without going into too much depth by distinguishing the difference between both network services in OpenStack, it might be crucial to identify how Sahara can handle the network operation in a Hadoop cluster using either Nova-network or neutron. By default, Sahara uses nova-network. However, we have configured in our RDO installation to use Neutron. This can be verified in the `/etc/sahara/sahara-api.conf` configuration file in the cloud controller:

```
...
use_neutron=True
...
```

Most importantly, Sahara requires SSH access to the instances of the Hadoop cluster once successfully spawned. To do so, Sahara will use either their fixed or floating IP.

By default, Sahara uses floating IP. This can be verified in the Sahara configuration file with the following directive:

```
...
use_floating_ips=True
...
```

 If using nova-network for OpenStack networking, make sure that `/etc/nova/nova.conf` has the configuration directive `auto_assign_floating_ip` set to `True`.

If the previous directive is set to `False`, Sahara will use the fixed IPs to access the instances. Hadoop instances can also gain floating IP addresses during the creation of the node group template in Sahara as the following:

In this case, all the instances spawned within that node group template will have a floating IP served from the public pool defined by the administrator.

To list the floating IP pool existing in OpenStack, issue the following command line:

```
# nova floating-ip-pool-list
```

 For more information on how to use floating IP in OpenStack, refer to the official OpenStack administration guide: `http://docs.openstack.org/user-guide/cli_manage_ip_addresses.html`.

Increasing data reliability

Block storage in OpenStack code named Cinder has resolved a few major issues that exist in the former OpenStack releases. Instead of counting on ephemeral storage, creating a persistent storage volume will prevent the deletion of data when the instance is terminated. Cinder API offers a full set of block storage management interface that allows creating, removing, resizing, attaching, and detaching volumes to instances. This is also the case for Sahara. It is possible to create and attach volumes to instances associated to a node group during cluster provisioning. This is a very fruitful feature from a reliability perspective since a Hadoop cluster relies on its HDFS.

Cinder includes a scheduler that schedules the location of new volumes based on a filter policy. Based on the highest weight backend, the cinder-scheduler will assign to it the creation of a new volume. From a performance perspective, the block storage service in OpenStack allows to define explicitly the locality of the volume instance. Several filters may exist within Cinder. In order to ensure the creation of the instance volumes on the same hypervisor as the guest host, Cinder provides `InstanceLocalityFilter`, which selects by default the storage backend located in the same physical host. A very pertinent example is the HDFS use case. A Hadoop environment may increase its data performance analysis and management by creating and attaching volumes to Hadoop instances within the same host as the hypervisor. In this case, every compute host should run the **cinder-volume** service. In addition, one physical machine must run the **cinder-scheduler** service in the cluster as shown in the next diagram:

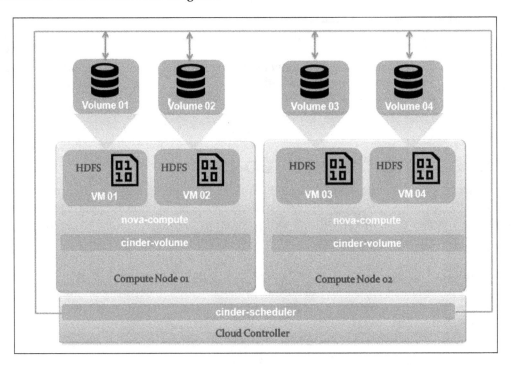

The next part of this chapter will guide you through a set of steps to enable data locality in Sahara:

1. It might be required to add `InstanceLocalityFilter` to the default schedulers' directive in the cinder configuration file as the following:

```
# nano /etc/cinder/cinder.conf
...
```

```
scheduler_default_filters = AvailabilityZoneFilter,CapacityFilter,
CapabilitiesFilter, InstanceLocalityFilter
...
```

2. Restart the Cinder service on the cloud controller:

   ```
   # openstack-service restart openstack-cinder-*
   ```

3. Log in to Horizon and create a new node group cluster within your plugin preference by selecting in the Storage location drop-down list the **Cinder Volume** option:

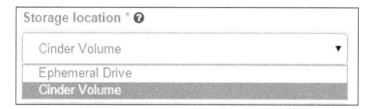

4. A new set of fields will appear in the same interface. Make sure to check **Volume local to instance** as the following:

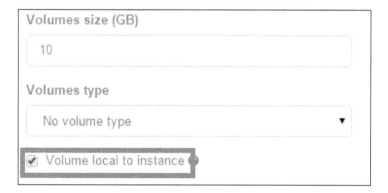

5. The volume instance locality feature will be enabled only for the node group in which it has been specified in the template. In this example, the previous Spark cluster has been edited in both the master and slave node groups template to support volume instance locality.

Once the cluster has been launched and instances are active, each volume should be created within the same host where the instance has been created. For example, spawning a Spark cluster within anti-affinity mode enabled will make sure that every instance will have an attached volume created in every compute node cn01 and cn02 respectively.

Summary

The main reason for Sahara's continuity support in OpenStack is the overwhelming features list implemented. The good modularity of the Sahara project and its integration in OpenStack facilitates the usage of more advanced configurations and performs more customizations. Although the previous chapters have covered the usage of Sahara plugins and how to provision a Hadoop cluster in no time, it misses a trivial feature that should be detailed in this chapter: high availability. The next chapter will discuss which Sahara plugins support the high-availability feature on cluster provisioning and how to configure it.

Hadoop High Availability Using Sahara

Ultimately, ensuring a high available system might need a large investment of time and expertise. Without a doubt, building a Hadoop cluster requires more crucial configuration steps in order to respond properly in the event of failure. At this point, installing and configuring manually a high available Hadoop cluster might be an error-prone process. In addition, adopting a HA solution in a Hadoop cluster needs more expertise on different processes that need a customized setup. The difficulty of such a setup might vary from one Hadoop plugin cluster to another. However, it is more practical to simplify the HA deployment setup using Sahara. This chapter will cover how to deploy easily a high available Hadoop cluster without going through any other third-party tool or solution. On the other hand, it is important to note that the latter setup is only limited to HDP and CDH plugins in Sahara.

HDP high-availability support

Designing and deploying a high-availability cluster generally is a complicated task. When it comes to the big data world, ensuring a running Hadoop cluster that responds efficiently to sudden failures might require a lot of expertise and remain complex to troubleshoot, maintain, and join failed nodes to the cluster manually. The HDP defines in its native Hadoop stack architecture a few approaches to undertake the Hadoop high-availability limitation. By ensuring the availability of the nodes that are running the master services in a Hadoop cluster, such as the NameNode, any other dependent service will be able to coordinate with other nodes to fail over by pausing specific services and start to recover the connection to the failed node. There are few alternatives to guarantee a successful NameNode failover, which can be depicted in two common use cases as the following:

- Using a VMware infrastructure (**vSphere**) by enabling the High Availability feature kit for the NameNode guest machines in the HDP cluster

- Using a Red Hat Enterprise solution by enabling the High Availability feature kit for the NameNode guest machines in the HDP cluster

The preceding HA alternatives are commonly adopted. However, other solutions may exist. To read more about HDP HA models using VMware and the Red Hat Enterprise solution, check the HortonWorks official website by following these links:

```
http://hortonworks.com/press-releases/hortonworks-
delivers-proven-high-availability-solution-for-apache-
hadoop/
```

```
http://hortonworks.com/blog/welcome-hortonworks-data-
platform-1-1/
```

Although the aforementioned solutions might satisfy a full high-availability Hadoop stack, it might be a long manual configuration process. In addition, using a specific commercial HA solution can be expensive and non free vendor lock-in. However, using Sahara, the solution can be less complicated and inexpensive. Starting from HDP 2.0.6 in the OpenStack Liberty release, it is possible to deploy a high-availability Hadoop cluster using the HDP plugin. This can be achieved by implementing a simple high-availability **Hadoop Distributed File System (HDFS)** on the NameNode in the cluster. The next diagram shows in detail how this can be achieved:

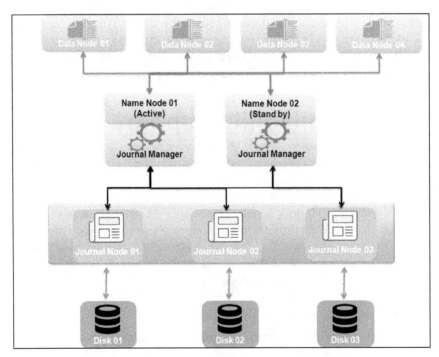

Minimum requirements for the HA Hadoop cluster in Sahara

The minimum high-availability setup requires at least the presence of two NameNodes, three JournalNodes, and three Zookeeper_Servers process nodes in different cluster nodes or servers. With this architecture, the NameNode is no longer presenting a **single point of failure** (**SPOF**). The NameNode starts to write its edits to a set of Journal Nodes. The idea uses simply a quorum Journal manager, which is a protocol that ensures the synchronization of edit commits between all the Journal Nodes. The Standby NameNode is in this case reading only the changes or edits from any of the replicas stored in the Journal Nodes and maintaining enough state to provide a fast failover if necessary. The automatic failover in this case will be ensured by the Zookeeper process nodes named **ZKFC** (short for **Zookeeper Failover Controllers**).

HA Hadoop cluster templates

The next wizard will demonstrate how to set up a high-availability HDP cluster using the Sahara API. The setup will include two NameNodes, at least three Journal Nodes, and at least three Zookeeper nodes. Note that the setup description associates every node to a separate process in the cluster. It might be possible to combine processes by node groups.

1. Create a first node group template called `DataNode_Template`, which will define the DataNode node process:

```
# nano DataNode_Template.json
{
    "plugin_name": "hdp",
    "hadoop_version": "2.0.6",
    "node_processes": [
        "DATANODE"
    ],
    "name": "datanode-pool",
    "flavor_id": "3",
    "auto_security_group": true
}
```

2. Upload the `datanode-pool` node group template:

```
# sahara node-group-template-create --json DataNode_Template.json
```

3. Create a second node group template called `journalnode-pool`, which will define the Journal node process:

```
{
    "plugin_name": "hdp",
    "hadoop_version": "2.0.6",
    "node_processes": [
        "JOURNALNODE"
    ],
    "name": "journalnode-pool",
    "flavor_id": "2",
    "auto_security_group": true
}
```

4. Upload the `journalnode-pool` node group template:

```
# sahara node-group-template-create --json Journal_Template.json
```

5. Create a third node group template called `ZK_Template`, which will define the Zookeeper node process:

```
{
    "plugin_name": "hdp",
    "hadoop_version": "2.0.6",
    "node_processes": [
        "ZOOKEEPER-SERVER"
    ],
    "name": "zookeeper-pool",
    "flavor_id": "2",
    "auto_security_group": true
}
```

6. Upload the `zookeeper_pool` node group template:

```
# sahara node-group-template-create --json ZK_Template.json
```

7. The next step requires defining the cluster template. The next template exposes exception a new directive to enable the high-availability feature in the HDP cluster denoted by the block "HDFSHA": {"hdfs.nnha": true } in the JSON template. If the HDFSHA property is missing, Sahara will throw the following error:

> Error: NameNode High Availability: JOURNALNODE can only be added when NameNode High Availability is enabled. Error ID: 56822eca-ef58-4d10-990e-2eb45c536f0b

8. The rest of the template includes the template for each node group created
    previously by pointing to the template ID for each one. Optionally, the
    template takes into account an additional YARN node and MAPR node
    processes within their associated pools 'yarn-pool' and 'mapr-pool'
    respectively as described next:

```
# nano hdp-ha-template.json
{
    "name": "HDP-HA-Template",
    "plugin_name": "hdp",
    "hadoop_version": "2.0.6",
    "cluster_configs": {
        "HDFSHA": {
                "hdfs.nnha": true
        }
    },
        "node_groups": [
        {
            "name": "namenode-pool",
            "node_group_template_id": "5f95e853-ca48-4826-
             af50-a035f04ae13b",
            "count": 2
        },
        {

            "name": "journal-pool",
            "node_group_template_id": "265c1c23-6b38-4556-
             ba19-221dc94b1591",
            "count": 3
        },
        {

            "name": "zookeeper-pool",
            "node_group_template_id": "89c25f11-c07d-41db-
             993f-ee85c2bb8590",
            "count": 3
        },
    {

            "name": "yarn-pool",
            "node_group_template_id": "aa95dcd6-042d-4833-
             ba65-fa3f740f65f0",
            "count": 1
        },
        {

            "name": "datanode-pool",
            "node_group_template_id": "1770d02c-9ac4-4351-
             aee7-ee081843a511",
            "count": 3
```

```
        },
    {
            "name": "mapr-pool",
            "node_group_template_id": "415b4076-5966-46a8-
            b414-db48be0d4acd",
            "count": 1
        }
    ]
}
```

9. Upload the cluster template as follows:

    ```
    # sahara --debug cluster-template-create --json hdp-cluster-
    template.json
    ```

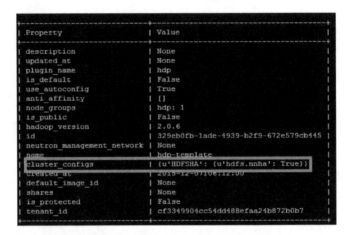

10. The cluster template is successfully uploaded within HDFS with the High
    Availability feature enabled as shown in Horizon:

11. Launch the cluster within the new cluster template:

12. The cluster will be spawned and it might take a while to be ready.

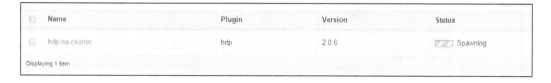

It might also be useful to check the status for each instance of the cluster in the instances tab in Horizon. Each instance of the HDP cluster will be named according to its role in the cluster as the following: HDP_HA_NAME-cluster-ROLE-ID where:

- **HDP_HA_NAME** : pp-hdp-ha

- **Cluster**: Default cluster key name

- **ROLE**: Which can be namenode-pool, journal-pool, zookeeper-pool, yarn-pool, datanode-pool, and mapr-pool

- **ID**: The number for each node by role defined in the cluster template

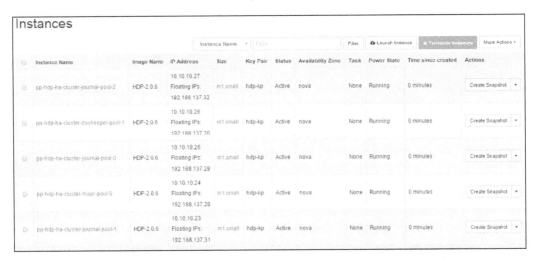

From the Horizon dashboard, it is possible to check the current number and state of the instances being built and spawned to form the HDP cluster. Note that the number of instances should reflect the number of HDP processes assigned by node group template in the previous steps based on the count parameter in the cluster template. The cluster will be entirely active and useful when all instances are spawned successfully.

If one of the nodes fails, the whole HA cluster must be launched again. Possible instance spawning errors might be the reason for non-sufficient resources such as RAM, CPU, or disk space. This has to be checked in the compute node(s) and their resources availability.

CDH high-availability support

The CDH 5.4.0 plugin allows the building of a high-availability CDH cluster through HDFS cluster groups. This can be achieved by setting up a YARN HA ResourceManager in Active/Standby mode architecture. The Sahara plugins deploys automatically the CDH cluster, and if HA enabled, ResourceManagers can fail over automatically through its failover controller or manually using the admin command-line interface. As shown in the next diagram, any active **ResourceManager** in the cluster needs to write its current states into ZooKeeper clusters. When the failure occurs, the **StandBy ResourceManager** will be promoted to be active and starts to load the **ResourceManager** state:

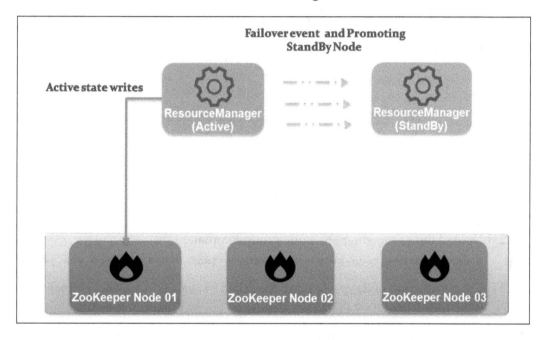

Like HDP, there are few requirements in order to support HA functionality in Sahara. Make sure to add an odd number of nodes running JOURNALNODE processes with at least a number of 3 per CDH cluster. Unlike HDP, it is not necessary to go through the cluster template and enable the HDFSHA option in the template file. Within CDH, the existence of the following process nodes in the cluster are enough to build a HA cluster as follows:

- At least three JOURNALNODE process nodes
- Zookeeper enabled on at least one cluster node

The next wizard will configure a HA HDFS cluster based on the Sahara CDH plugin. It is important to enable the anti-affinity feature on the NameNode and SecondaryNode process nodes while creating the cluster template. This will ensure that both of the node processes will run on different physical hosts.

> Enabling anti-affinity for a specific process will guarantee that particular process will be launched in any virtual machines located in different hardware hosts. The scheduler will make sure that that process will not run in the same hypervisor machine.

1. Create a first node group template called DataNode_Template, which will define the HDFS_DataNode node process:

```
# nano DataNode_Template.json
{
    "plugin_name": "cdh",
    "hadoop_version": "5.4.0",
    "node_processes": [
        "HDFS_DATANODE"
    ],
    "name": "datanode-pool",
    "flavor_id": "1",
    "auto_security_group": true
}
```

2. Upload the datanode-pool node group template:

```
# sahara node-group-template-create --json DataNode_Template.json
```

3. Create a second node group template called NameNode_Template, which will define the name node process:

```
{
    "plugin_name": "cdh",
    "hadoop_version": "5.4.0",
    "node_processes": [
        "HDFS_NAMENODE"
    ],
    "name": "namenode-pool",
    "flavor_id": "1",
    "auto_security_group": true
}
```

4. Upload the `namenode-pool` node group template:

```
# sahara node-group-template-create --json NameNode _Template.json
```

5. Create a third node group template called `YARN_Template`. For the sake of simplicity, this template will sum all the YARN processes as the following:

```
{
    "plugin_name": "cdh",
    "hadoop_version": "5.4.0",
    "node_processes": [
        "YARN_JOBHISTORY",
        "YARN_RESOURCEMANAGER",
        "YARN_NODEMANAGER"
    ],
    "name": "yarn-pool",
    "flavor_id": "2",
    "auto_security_group": true
}
```

6. Upload the `yarn-pool` node group template:

```
# sahara node-group-template-create --json YARN_Template.json
```

7. The next group template will be created called `RM_Template`. This template will enquire in the first place the `ResourceManager` role as well as the `HDFS_SecondaryNameNode` role as follows:

```
{
    "plugin_name": "cdh",
    "hadoop_version": "5.4.0",
    "node_processes": [
        "CLOUDERA_MANAGER",
        "HDFS_SECONDARYNAMENODE",
    ],
    "name": "rm-pool",
    "flavor_id": "2",
    "auto_security_group": true
}
```

8. Upload the `rm-pool` node group template:

```
# sahara node-group-template-create --json RM_Template.json
```

9. To accomplish a HA HDFS setup for the CDH cluster, it still needed to join a cluster of JOURNAL processes nodes and a Zookeeper process node. It might be possible to merge both roles in the same group template. In order to mimic a production environment, the next template will only include a Zookeeper group as follows:

```
{
    "plugin_name": "cdh",
    "hadoop_version": "5.4.0",
    "node_processes": [
        "ZOOKEEPER_SERVER"
    ],
    "name": "zookeeper-pool",
    "flavor_id": "2",
    "auto_security_group": true
}
```

10. Upload the zookeeper-pool node group template:

```
# sahara node-group-template-create --json ZK_Template.json
```

11. The last template will include the Journal node group template as follows:

```
{
    "plugin_name": "cdh",
    "hadoop_version": "5.4.0",
    "node_processes": [
        "HDFS_JOURNALNODE"
    ],
    "name": "journal-pool",
    "flavor_id": "2",
    "auto_security_group": true
}
```

12. Upload the `journal-pool` node group template:

```
# sahara node-group-template-create --json JN_Template.json
```

13. The next step will specify the cluster template that will include one node per each group template created previously excepting the `journal_pool` template that will take into account three nodes. The cluster template will include the node group template ID for each created in the previous steps. It is easier to collect the ID output for each node group template by simply running the following Sahara command line:

```
# sahara node-group-template-list
```

14. NameNode and SecondaryNameNode will be set into anti-affinity nodes as the following:

```
# nano cdh-ha-template.json
{
    "name": "cdh-ha-template",
    "plugin_name": "cdh",
    "hadoop_version": "5.4.0",
    "anti_affinity": ["HDFS_NAMENODE","HDFS_SECONDARYNAMENODE"],
        "node_groups": [
        {
            "name": "namenode-pool",
            "node_group_template_id": "85c72dcb-1fb5-49a2-
            8ad0-be1fcfdf30f2",
            "count": 1
        },
        {
            "name": "yarn-pool",
            "node_group_template_id": "c9b5e596-ecbe-4b4b-
            a075-5098a0a7780f",
            "count": 1
        },
        {
            "name": "rm-pool",
            "node_group_template_id": "2cc57e30-e91a-4d31-
            8c91-369a3986d733",
            "count": 1
        },
        {
            "name": "zookeeper-pool",
            "node_group_template_id": "24fc66eb-c189-4fb8-
            8bda-9e64963bae58",
            "count": 1
        },
        {
            "name": "journal-pool",
            "node_group_template_id": "8cf2979a-48d7-4251-
            9ca3-f1a2efa583bd",
            "count": 3
        }
    ]
}
```

15. Upload the `cdh-ha-template` cluster template:

```
# sahara cluster-template-create --json Cluster_Template.json
```

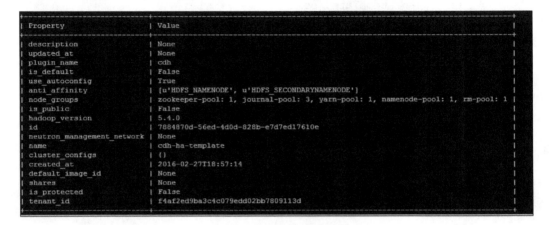

```
+------------------------------+--------------------------------------------------------------------------------+
| Property                     | Value                                                                          |
+------------------------------+--------------------------------------------------------------------------------+
| description                  | None                                                                           |
| updated_at                   | None                                                                           |
| plugin_name                  | cdh                                                                            |
| is_default                   | False                                                                          |
| use_autoconfig               | True                                                                           |
| anti_affinity                | [u'HDFS_NAMENODE', u'HDFS_SECONDARYNAMENODE']                                   |
| node_groups                  | zookeeper-pool: 1, journal-pool: 3, yarn-pool: 1, namenode-pool: 1, rm-pool: 1 |
| is_public                    | False                                                                          |
| hadoop_version               | 5.4.0                                                                          |
| id                           | 7884870d-56ed-4d0d-828b-e7d7ed17610e                                           |
| neutron_management_network   | None                                                                           |
| name                         | cdh-ha-template                                                                |
| cluster_configs              | {}                                                                             |
| created_at                   | 2016-02-27T18:57:14                                                            |
| default_image_id             | None                                                                           |
| shares                       | None                                                                           |
| is_protected                 | False                                                                          |
| tenant_id                    | f4af2ed9ba3c4c079edd02bb7809113d                                               |
+------------------------------+--------------------------------------------------------------------------------+
```

16. Launch the cluster within the new cluster template:

The new CDH cluster will be spawned by building all the configured instances in the cluster template mentioned previously:

It might also be useful to check the status for each instance of the cluster in the instances tab in Horizon. Each instance of the CDH cluster will have named according to its role in the cluster as the following: CDH_HA_NAME-Cluster-ROLE-ID where:

- **CDH_HA_NAME** : cdh-ha
- **Cluster**: Default cluster key name
- **ROLE**: Which can be namenode-pool, yarn-pool, rm-pool, zookeeper-pool, journal-pool
- **ID**: The number for each node by role defined in the cluster template

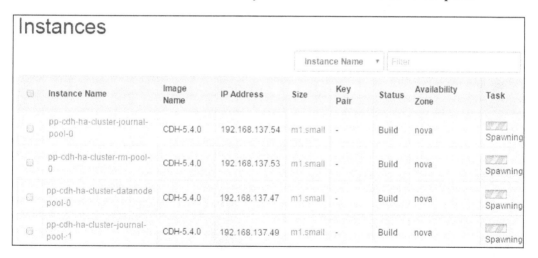

Summary

A successful Hadoop cluster design comes from its availability when one or many of its nodes fails for any reason. It becomes essential to ensure a high available Hadoop cluster before moving to production. By virtue of its simplicity, Sahara facilitates an HA Hadoop setup with minimum manual configuration. The chapter has introduced how to launch a high available Hadoop cluster based on few requirements settings. Although the current version supports HA on HDFS only for the HDP and CDH plugins, the Sahara project keeps growing and covering more advanced features for other plugins. By the end of this chapter, most of the advanced functionalities provided by Sahara have been covered. On the other hand, within every OpenStack release, more bugs are being fixed and many new features are being improved.

7
Troubleshooting

OpenStack exposes different components and services that communicate between each other. Installing and running an OpenStack cluster can be an error-prone process and one or several services might fail to start. We have seen in *Chapter 1, The Essence of Big Data in the Cloud* the integration of the Sahara project into the OpenStack ecosystem. Sahara depends directly on many OpenStack services to run properly and generate the expected results. Additionally, it was concluded that Sahara communicates with other OpenStack services by means of APIs including compute, image, storage, orchestration, and network services. With this in mind, it might be crucial to take a look at some details and highlight how things run under the hood. Although *Chapter 2, Integrating OpenStack Sahara* describes how to install OpenStack and integrate Sahara in a test environment, going to production may generate unexpected errors that need to be addressed. As discussed in *Chapter 2, Integrating OpenStack Sahara*, we have installed OpenStack using RDO. By virtue of its simple installation in a small test environment, this example should be usable to demonstrate the functionalities of Sahara, but it is not advised to use RDO for an OpenStack production environment.

Troubleshooting OpenStack

To figure out exactly what could be wrong in an OpenStack cluster, you should go through a certain number of steps. With several moving services that run OpenStack, troubleshooting a specific component should be addressed independently. For example, the Sahara service might generate a generic error while launching a cluster. The best and fastest way to work around such a problem is to address directly the root cause.

OpenStack debug tool

OpenStack provides an amazing command-line utility allowing the checking of the status of services that should run on every OpenStack node as specified during the packstack installation. For example, to check the status of the OpenStack services running on the cloud controller node, run the `openstack-status` command line as follows:

```
# openstack-status
```

```
== Nova services ==
openstack-nova-api:                         active
openstack-nova-cert:                        active
openstack-nova-compute:                     inactive
openstack-nova-network:                     inactive  (disabled on boot)
openstack-nova-scheduler:                   active
openstack-nova-conductor:                   active
== Glance services ==
openstack-glance-api:                       active
openstack-glance-registry:                  active
== Keystone service ==
openstack-keystone:                         active    (disabled on boot)
== Horizon service ==
openstack-dashboard:                        active
== neutron services ==
neutron-server:                             active
neutron-dhcp-agent:                         active
neutron-l3-agent:                           active
neutron-metadata-agent:                     active
neutron-openvswitch-agent:                  active
== Swift services ==
openstack-swift-proxy:                      active
openstack-swift-account:                    active
openstack-swift-container:                  active
openstack-swift-object:                     active
== Cinder services ==
openstack-cinder-api:                       active
openstack-cinder-scheduler:                 active
openstack-cinder-volume:                    active
openstack-cinder-backup:                    active
== Ceilometer services ==
openstack-ceilometer-api:                   active
openstack-ceilometer-central:               active
openstack-ceilometer-compute:               active
openstack-ceilometer-collector:             active
openstack-ceilometer-alarm-notifier:        active
openstack-ceilometer-alarm-evaluator:       active
openstack-ceilometer-notification:          active
== Heat services ==
openstack-heat-api:                         active
openstack-heat-api-cfn:                     inactive  (disabled on boot)
openstack-heat-api-cloudwatch:              inactive  (disabled on boot)
openstack-heat-engine:                      active
== Support services ==
mysqld:                                     active    (disabled on boot)
openvswitch:                                active
dbus:                                       active
target:                                     active
rabbitmq-server:                            active
memcached:                                  active
```

The previous command-line output illustrates the following:

- `openstack-nova-compute`: Inactive since the nova service is running in a different compute node.

- `openstack-keystone`: Is active but it is not enabled on boot. This will raise a service authentication error when restarting the OpenStack cloud controller node. Users and the rest of the OpenStack services will not be able to send API requests since the keystone will appear as not running in the next boot. It is important to enable it on boot as follows:

  ```
  # chkconfig --level 2345 openstack-keystone on
  ```

- `mysqld`: Is active but it is not enabled on boot. On the next boot of the cloud controller, all services of OpenStack will not be able to save or retrieve any service attribute. It is important to enable it on boot as follows:

  ```
  #  chkconfig --level 2345 mysqld on
  ```

Another useful tool allowing tracing individually the status of any enabled OpenStack service is `openstack-service`. For example, it is possible to check the status of the Sahara service as follows:

```
# openstack-service status openstack-sahara

MainPID=22086 Id=openstack-sahara-api.service ActiveState=active

MainPID=22087 Id=openstack-sahara-engine.service ActiveState=active
```

Troubleshooting SELinux

One of the major issues that can prevent OpenStack from running properly is SELinux running on Fedora and RHEL. SELinux is enabled by default and is a mandatory access control mechanism implemented in the CentOS kernel. A new CentOS box freshly installed will require a few adjustments in the kernel security layer in order to allow certain operations on each operating system object such as processes, files, and file descriptors.

 To read more about SELinux, refer to the official CentOS wiki page:
https://wiki.centos.org/HowTos/SELinux

It is possible that certain services in OpenStack will not work properly because of the SELinux context. For example, if Sahara is configured to use object storage for input/ output elastic data processing, it is possible to end up with the following error on Horizon while creating a container in Swift:

Error: Unable to retrieve container list. ✕

Although the OpenStack service command-line tool shows that Swift is up and running, a slightly different way of tracing the previous error can be checked in SELinux exceptions. SELinux can run in three different modes:

- **Enforcing**: A mode enabling the SELinux security policy and access to resources is denied.

- **Permissive**: A mode permitting operations on resources but enforcing warning and logging actions.

- **Disabled**: SELinux is disabled. No security policy is enforced or logged.

 Disabling SELinux can be performed for test purposes. In a production environment, it is not recommended to disable it entirely; however, it is still possible to set it to permissive mode for troubleshooting reasons.

In our case, file access for the object service is forbidden. This can be verified on the audit log file, /var/log/audit/audit.log.

```
# tail -f /var/log/audit/audit.log

type=AVC msg=audit(1457842892.832:3561689): avc:  denied  { unlink }
for  pid=19475 comm=»swift-container» name=»object.recon» dev=»dm-0»
ino=136255612 scontext=system_u:system_r:swift_t:s0 tcontext=unconfined_u
:object_r:var_t:s0 tclass=file

type=SYSCALL msg=audit(1457842892.832:3561689): arch=c000003e syscall=82
success=yes exit=0 a0=2279830 a1=227ae30 a2=7ff4b2664fa8 a3=3 items=0
ppid=1 pid=19475 auid=4294967295 uid=1002 gid=1003 euid=1002 suid=1002
fsuid=1002 egid=1003 sgid=1003 fsgid=1003 tty=(none) ses=4294967295
comm="swift-object-re" exe="/usr/bin/python2.7" subj=system_u:system_r:sw
ift_t:s0 key=(null)
```

The exception logged in permissive mode can be interpreted using the message code highlighted in bold, **1457842892.832**. Using the adit2why command line, it might be possible to get recommendations on how to allow access to the Swift resources as follows:

```
# grep 1457842892.832 /var/log/audit/audit.log | audit2why

type=AVC msg=audit(1457842892.832:3561689): avc:  denied  { unlink }
for  pid=19475 comm="swift-container" name="container.recon" dev="dm-0"
ino=136255612 scontext=system_u:system_r:swift_t:s0 tcontext=unconfined_u
:object_r:var_t:s0 tclass=file

        Was caused by:
            Missing type enforcement (TE) allow rule.

            You can use audit2allow to generate a loadable   module
to allow this access.
```

A rapid workaround of the file restrictions of Swift container resources, it is possible to modify the Swift file label as the following:

```
# chcon -v --type=swift_t /var/cache/swift/container.recon

changing security context of '/var/cache/swift/container.recon'
```

Troubleshooting identity

Without keystone, different components of OpenStack will not be able to talk to one another. One of the most frequent errors in keystone is the following:

```
Unable to communicate with identity service:  No route to host.
```

This error appears when the keystone service client is not able to contact the identity service. Checking keystone from the Openstack service list can be verified as follows:

```
# openstack-service status openstack-keystone

MainPID=8969 Id=openstack-keystone.service ActiveState=active
```

Since the service is up and running, the problem can be escalated to firewall settings. Basically, keystone needs to allow TCP traffic on ports 5000 and 35357. The cloud controller should listen to both ports as follows:

```
# netstat -ntpl | grep -E '35357|5000'
tcp        0      0 0.0.0.0:5000            0.0.0.0:*
LISTEN      8969/python2
tcp        0      0 0.0.0.0:35357           0.0.0.0:*
LISTEN      8969/python2
```

For example, while integrating Sahara to the OpenStack environment, a new keystone endpoint should be added to Sahara. At the first attempt, the following error can be obtained when trying to run the data processing service:

```
publicURL endpoint for data-processing service not found
```

Make sure that the Sahara endpoint exists on the keystone service catalogue but listing the services on the OpenStack cloud controller as follows:

Get the data-processing service ID:

```
# keystone service-list | grep data-processing
| 0c2429b825a64e89b01e6896da4f2570 |   sahara  | data-processing |
Sahara Data Processing    |
```

Check the correctness of the data-processing endpoint:

```
# keystone endpoint-list | grep 0c2429b825a64e89b01e6896da4f2570
| 2f73d67b70b44c21bd41c92cdfae43db | RegionOne
|  http://185.34.220.246:8386/v1.1/%(tenant_id)
s  |   http://185.34.220.246:8386/v1.1/%(tenant_id)
s  |  http://185.34.220.246:8386/v1.1/%(tenant_id)s |
0c2429b825a64e89b01e6896da4f2570 |
```

Troubleshooting networking

Networking in OpenStack is a special component among other services in the whole ecosystem. Specifically, since Neutron has been used to manage networking configuration for the Sahara cluster instances, it is essential to have an insight on flows for traffic instances when launching a Hadoop cluster, for example.

One of most important basics of networking when using Neutron is the network namespace. This is where the instance network is defined and isolated from the host-level networking. Assuming the existence of only one tenant in the OpenStack environment, the following command line lists two namespaces:

```
# ip netns
qrouter-80944171-f753-4b50-8336-6d5ff74acd1a
qdhcp-fbf94e05-3d97-48c2-83c4-a77a0d2ffea0
```

`qdhcp-ID` is a namespace created to manage DHCP for instances in the private network in Neutron whereas `qrouter-ID` defines the router namespace that connects the instance to interface the external network and reach the Internet, for example. A few tools can be used to check the connection between instances in the same cluster. Additionally, using namespace command lines might help to trace the traffic from the Internet to the instances and vice versa. For example, running some Hadoop clusters using Sahara requires access to the Internet to download specific packages. In case of a connectivity issue with the external network, try to trace traffic traversing in more than one namespace.

The next command line lists different bridges and ports configured by Neutron:

```
# ovs-vsctl show
```

Most importantly, when looking to the port and bridge list, there are quite a few chances for the traffic to get lost. A step-by-step network troubleshooting practice can be tracked down by diagnosing the following points:

- Check security groups for each instance
- Check ICMP is allowed in the security groups to test using the ping command line
- Check if ping works from the qdhcp and qrouter namespaces
- Filter traffic on the virtual router interface, `br-int` and `br-ext`, using `tcpdump`
- Filter traffic from the router to get to the instance on the physical interface using `br-tun`

Troubleshooting data processing

As a very rough rule of thumb, troubleshooting issues with Sahara or any other component in OpenStack should be seen as a whole ecosystem where many other services could be running in an unexpected status. Therefore, Sahara will not be able to function properly. Covering all issues in OpenStack could fill an entire book; however, it might be essential to have a good understanding of its ecosystem. On the other hand, the data processing service may face a few problems while creating a Hadoop or Spark cluster, or when launching jobs.

Debugging Sahara

The Sahara command-line client's tools support the `--debug` option. This is very useful to show the execution of the Curl commands of each API call to the Sahara endpoint in OpenStack. For example, the debug option can be used to check the accessibility of the client to the endpoint by getting more details as follows:

```
# sahara --debug cluster-list
DEBUG (session:198) REQ: curl -g -i -X GET http:// 10.10.10.47:5000/v2.0
-H "Accept: application/json" -H "User-Agent: python-keystoneclient"
INFO (connectionpool:203) Starting new HTTP connection (1): 10.10.10.47
DEBUG (connectionpool:383) "GET /v2.0 HTTP/1.1" 200 340
DEBUG (session:215) RESP: [200] content-length: 340 vary: X-Auth-Token
connection: keep-alive date: Sun, 13 Mar 2016 22:18:04 GMT content-type:
application/json x-openstack-request-id: req-51dab55b-83c8-44f6-bfe6-
6f24ddbf3d4b
```

The debug option will also return a detailed JSON response of a list of clusters available in Sahara. The user will be able to trace how the connection is being performed when issuing the client command line and check further the status of accessibility of the endpoint.

For example, when the Sahara endpoint is not configured properly or its configuration files have been updated, the previous command line could generate the following exception:

```
...
INFO (connectionpool:203) Starting new HTTP connection (1): 122.55.47.11
DEBUG (shell:716) Unable to establish connection to
http://10.0.47.28:8386/v1.1/f4af2ed9ba3c4c079edd02bb7809113d/clusters
Traceback (most recent call last):
...
```

The previous debug message demonstrates that it might be an endpoint issue. In this case, either the IP of the host running Sahara is set incorrectly or it does not exist. This can be fixed by checking the host directive in the sahara.conf file and correct the IP address to point to the right host. After restarting the Sahara service and loading the right settings, the debug message will return a successful API response as shown earlier in this section.

Logging Sahara

Like most of the standard services in Linux/Unix systems, logs might be written and saved under the /var/log directory. A host running any OpenStack service stores its logs by defaults under /var/log/SERVICE_NAME_DIRECTORY where SERVICE_NAME_ DIRECTORY can be nova, glance, keystone, cinder, swift, neutron, ceilometer, heat, and sahara. Note that depending on the Linux distribution used for the OpenStack installation, log files for the OpenStack dashboard might reside in the following locations:

- **Fedora distribution**: /var/log/httpd
- **Debian distribution**: /var/log/apache2

On the other hand, instances spawned as a result of launching clusters in Sahara will place their logs in the compute nodes under /var/lib/nova/instances/instance-ID/.

For example, it is possible to check the status of spawning a new instance within a Hadoop cluster by tailing the console.log files generated by the nova service in the compute node:

```
# tail -f /var/lib/nova/instances/2e48bf98-cc46-4449-bf36-4c1a90d74190/
console.log

ec2: 256 82:92:aa:f7:00:87:69:19:81:af:ff:28:9c:7a:bd:eb   root@
sparkcluster-pp-spark-slave-node-001 (ED25519)

ec2: 2048 11:31:f8:3a:e1:a6:9b:26:fc:b2:c8:7c:eb:19:70:59   root@
sparkcluster-pp-spark-slave-node-001 (RSA)

. . . .

-----BEGIN SSH HOST KEY KEYS-----

. . . .

-----END SSH HOST KEY KEYS-----

Cloud-init v. 0.7.5 finished at Sun, 13 Mar 2016 22:12:21 +0000.
Datasource DataSourceEc2.  Up 722.55 seconds
```

Sahara has satisfactory logging messages and may pinpoint the root cause of the problem when facing an error message either from Horizon or from the command line.

This holds true when messages thrown in the Sahara log files look meaningful at first glance. For example, launching a new cluster in Sahara can be traced either for Horizon or from the `sahara-engine` log file. However, the user interface might not be helpful to trace every cluster status. Keeping an eye on the log file gives a bright insight on which stage the cluster is at. Take a look at the `sahara-engine` log file:

```
2016-03-13 22:58:25.732 18563 INFO sahara.main [-] Sahara engine started

...

2016-03-13 22:59:32.392 18563 INFO sahara.utils.cluster [req-4f321c5d-
f23e-47b3-bbaf-86f8f0528196 ] [instance: none, cluster: 760a56a3-
8a62-4ee6-9018-e07403bb07b7] Cluster status has been changed. New
status=InfraUpdating

2016-03-13 22:59:32.783 18563 INFO sahara.utils.cluster [req-4f321c5d-
f23e-47b3-bbaf-86f8f0528196 ] [instance: none, cluster: 760a56a3-
8a62-4ee6-9018-e07403bb07b7] Cluster status has been changed. New
status=Spawning

2016-03-13 22:59:35.628 18563 INFO sahara.utils.cluster [req-4f321c5d-
f23e-47b3-bbaf-86f8f0528196 ] [instance: none, cluster: 760a56a3-
8a62-4ee6-9018-e07403bb07b7] Cluster status has been changed. New
status=Waiting

2016-03-13 23:00:04.793 18563 INFO sahara.service.direct_engine [req-
4f321c5d-f23e-47b3-bbaf-86f8f0528196 ] [instance: none, cluster:
760a56a3-8a62-4ee6-9018-e07403bb07b7] All instances are active

2016-03-13 23:00:10.170 18563 INFO sahara.service.engine [req-4f321c5d-
f23e-47b3-bbaf-86f8f0528196 ] [instance: none, cluster: 760a56a3-8a62-
4ee6-9018-e07403bb07b7] All instances have IPs assigned
```

Obviously, the last status of the cluster was in Waiting status. That makes it imperative to take into account the behavior of clusters created within Sahara. For example, when the Waiting status of the cluster takes longer than expected, there is a strong chance of ending up with a timeout exception. In the current status, Sahara makes sure that all instances infrastructures resources including networking and storage are set properly for the cluster instances. Before starting the cluster, Sahara should make sure that the instances of the cluster are able to communicate between each other by generating a host file in each of them. Each instance should be able to access other instances within the same cluster using the hostname. A common issue that might occur is when Waiting status ends up with the following error:

```
...

TimeoutException: 'Operation with name 'Wait for instance accessibility'

...
```

A workaround to this exception is to verify that Sahara is able to generate the `/etc/hosts` file as well as updating the `authorized_keys` file per created instance.

Troubleshooting missing services

Each Hadoop cluster requires a minimum number of processes that should be checked during the creation of the template cluster. Within more complicated and advanced cluster settings, it might be painful to memorize every cluster processes list. The good news is that Sahara is able to detect any missed process during the launch of the cluster creation. The next log output shows a missing service during the launch of a Hadoop cluster:

```
Validation Error occurred: error_code=400, error_message=Cluster is
missing a service: YARN

Error ID: 0e3f2340-b354-483c-894c-0d037e7d9770, error_name=MISSING_
SERVICE
```

The logging message is meaningful. Sahara checks before launching the cluster the presence of the required services through a validation service list. Once a service is missed, a validation error will be raised and the cluster template must be reconfigured.

Troubleshooting cluster creation

Few exceptions cannot be logged within a clear message while provisioning a new cluster in Sahara. Thus, it is necessary to go through other log files generated by OpenStack services. As discussed previously, Sahara depends directly on other OpenStack components. Ultimately, it might be hard to pinpoint directly the service causing the issue. As a good practice, it is recommended to use a logging solution such as **Logstash** and perform search indexing on error messages and exceptions using **Kibana**. This way, any error Sahara message can be tracked within the same timestamp on other log service files of OpenStack.

 To learn more about the integration of Logstash and Kibana with OpenStack, check the following URL: `http://docs.openstack.org/infra/system-config/logstash.html`

A common indirect exception generated by Sahara log files can escalate the problem to the compute service, for example. By going through the nova compute log files, the following exception is shown:

```
...

No valid host was found. There are not enough hosts available.

...
```

Obviously, Sahara sent a request to Nova to create a certain number of instances. The API response from Nova did not reach the Sahara endpoint. The compute service was kept busy to figure out how much resources are left to fill the request needs. Basically, this is a common issue when there are no resources left such as CPU and RAM in the compute or hypervisor host. In addition, when running nova-compute on a virtual machine, the nova.conf file should be configured to use qemu.

When using anti-affinity while creating clusters in Sahara, make sure that more than one compute host exists in the OpenStack environment. This will inform Nova to spawn a new instance within the anti-affinity service enabled in a different compute node that will be tackled by nova-scheduler.

Troubleshooting user quota

A very common issue that a user might face when reaching the OpenStack predefined limits is the user quota. For example, launching a Hadoop cluster in HA as demonstrated in *Chapter 6, Hadoop High Availability Using Sahara* could fire up a quota exceeded error in the Horizon dashboard, for example, as follows:

> Error: Quota exceeded for Instance:
> Requested 12, but available 10 Error
> ID: 09b264e3-194e-488c-a2b4-
> aa8eb6d50e5f

Obvisouly, the error message helps to pinpoint the root cause of the failure while launching a Hadoop cluster. However, it is more important to overcome such a problem by going through the Sahara log files.

```
# tail -f /var/log/sahara/sahara-engine.log
```

```
ERROR sahara.service.ops [req-e34ee343-173a-0033-f3e2-3922-cb3e556eb2534]
[....] Error during operating on cluster (reason: Heat stack failed with
status Resource Create failed: resources.yarn-pool: OverQuotaClient:
resources[0].resources.pp=cdh-ha-cluster-yarn-pool-1a0fa8c5: Quota
exceeded for resources: ['security_group_rule'])
```

The previous truncked error log message shows clearly that the creation of the CDH cluster failed .The error occurs because the Sahara client has exceeded the request limits of the Security Groups resources for each node newly spawned and joined the cluster. Some other variants of the same error message can show up for CPU, RAM, floating IP, volumes, and instance count. In this case, it is possible to tune the quota limits by modifiying the following directives in the /etc/nova/nova.conf file:

```
max_cores=150
cpu_allocation_ratio=16.0
```

```
quota_cores=150
quota_instances=750
quota_floating_ips=1000
quota_metadata_items=250
quota_security_group_rules=100
quota_security_groups=100
quota_volumes=50
```

 It is also possible to take advantage of the overprovisioing functionality by changing `skip_isolated_core_check` from `false` to `true`. To read more about overprovisioining and overcommitment in OpenStack, check this out: `http://docs.openstack.org/openstack-ops/content/compute_nodes.html`

Troubleshooting cluster scaling

A very interesting point about Sahara is its capability to detect a misconfiguration of a Hadoop cluster before launching it. As was demonstrated in *Chapter 5, Discovering Advanced Features with Sahara*, Sahara checks for each cluster template the existence of the minimum requirements that allow a Hadoop/Spark cluster to run such as the process types and their occurrence per cluster. Moreover, scaling a cluster in Sahara also sticks to a standard rule that does not allow any specific node to join within the same running processes to the existing cluster. For example, the following error message does not prove a state of failure of the cluster function but it prevents creating a new instance that will scale the existing Hadoop cluster by adding a new 'namenode' and 'master'. Scaling with this cluster will happen only with the node running the 'datanode' and 'slave' processes.

> **Error:** Chosen node group SparkMaster cannot be scaled : Spark plugin cannot scale nodegroup with processes: namenode datanode master slave Error ID: bdf0632c-9787-4ec9-8ae2-6c32ff3a605d

In order to take advantage of scaling in Sahara, it is considered a best practise to separate processes that need to scale in different instances.

Troubleshooting cluster access

Obviously, every instance within a cluster created by Sahara should be able to communicate between each other. The Sahara service must be able to log to every cluster node. It is always a good practice to refer to the log file output generated by the `sahara-engine` log file to get more details. Before preparing the cluster, Sahara should use SSH to access every node. At some point, a common issue could occur when Sahara tries to run any command as follows:

```
# tail /var/log/sahara/sahara-engine.log

...

DEBUG sahara.service.engine [-] Can't login to node cluster-pp-spark-master-node-001 10.10.10.45,

reason SSHException: Error reading SSH protocol banner _is_accessible /
usr/lib/python2.7/site-packages/sahara/service/engine.py:128

...
```

Before testing the SSH connection to the instances created, it is advised to check the following in order:

- Check security groups associated with every instance
- Check the SSH connection to every instance of the cluster via neutron namespaces
- Check how Sahara is configured to run commands on instances

Assuming that security groups are set by default allowing TCP traffic on port 22, it is possible to list the namespaces created by Neutron:

```
# ip netns
qrouter-80944171-f753-4b50-8336-6d5ff74acd1a
qdhcp-fbf94e05-3d97-48c2-83c4-a77a0d2ffea0
```

Using the `qrouter-ID` namespace, we can try to connect to one of the instances created by Sahara as follows:

```
# ip netns exec qrouter-80944171-f753-4b50-8336-6d5ff74acd1a
 ssh -i key.pem ubuntu@10.10.10.45
Warning: Permanently added '10.10.10.45' (ECDSA) to the list of known hosts.
Welcome to Ubuntu 14.04.3 LTS (GNU/Linux 3.13.0-65-generic x86_64)
ubuntu@cluster-pp-spark-master-node-001:~$
```

When connecting to the instance, it is possible to filter traffic to check any SSH packets are hitting the virtual interface of the virtual machine. In this case, Sahara is attempting to connect to the instance via SSH and expecting to see at least traffic coming to port 22:

```
ubuntu@cluster-pp-spark-master-node-001:~$ sudo tcpdump -i eth0 port 22
listening on eth0, link-type EN10MB (Ethernet), capture size 65535 bytes
```

Obviously, the Sahara service is not able to open any SSH connection to its cluster instances. The next part will require a complete review of how Sahara was configured to send commands. Basically, it could be execution rights issues. Thus, checking the Sahara processes on the cloud controller box will clarify the situation:

```
# ps -aux | grep sahara
sahara    18562  2.2  0.7 498212 116800 ?        Ss   Mar13    7:24 /usr/
bin/python2 /usr/bin/sahara-api --config-file /etc/sahara/sahara.conf
sahara    18563  3.1  0.6 495216 113780 ?        Ss   Mar13   10:23 /usr/
bin/python2 /usr/bin/sahara-engine --config-file /etc/sahara/sahara.conf
```

It is clearly stated that Sahara processes are run by a user called sahara. In this case, the Sahara service will need to launch commands by activating its root wrapper on the configuration file. Using the openstack-config command line, root wrapper directives can be set as follows:

```
# openstack-config --set /etc/sahara/sahara.conf DEFAULT use_rootwrap
True

# openstack-config --set /etc/sahara/sahara.conf DEFAULT rootwrap_command
"sudo sahara-rootwrap /etc/sahara/rootwrap.conf"
```

Make sure that the sahara-rootwrap file exists under /etc/sudoers/ as mentioned in the previous command line with the following content:

```
# cat /etc/sudoers.d/sahara-rootwrap
sahara ALL=(root) NOPASSWD: /usr/bin/sahara-rootwrap /etc/sahara/
rootwrap.conf *
```

This will allow Sahara to run a command as root without any permissions problems.

After making any proper changes, make sure to restart the service as follows:

```
# openstack-service restart openstack-sahara
```

The next launch of the cluster will show SSH traffic flowing in one of the cluster instances from the Sahara server as the following:

```
ubuntu@cluster-pp-spark-master-node-001:~$ sudo tcpdump -i eth0 port 22

listening on eth0, link-type EN10MB (Ethernet), capture size 65535 bytes

04:25:09.518500 IP 10.10.10.1.58419 > 10.10.10.45.ssh: Flags [.], ack
1158772, win 1399, options [nop,nop,TS val 4177511753 ecr 489268], length
0

04:25:09.519506 IP 10.10.10.45.ssh > 10.10.10.1.58419: Flags [P.], seq
1158772:1158808, ack 721, win 284, options [nop,nop,TS val 489271 ecr
4177511753]

...
```

Summary

This chapter has demonstrated how to resolve a few common issues that might occur when installing and configuring Sahara in OpenStack. This makes it imperative to understand how things in OpenStack work under the hood. Troubleshooting Sahara in OpenStack depends on the state of other services such as compute, storage, network, image, identity, and the orchestration service. Thus, it is essential to keep an eye on logs for different components of OpenStack when operating on Sahara. Keep using command-line tools provided by OpenStack to check quickly the activity of its Sahara service. It is also fruitful to track logs and trace error messages using an easy tool such as Logstash and Kibana in a production environment.

By tackling this troubleshooting chapter, our Sahara journey in OpenStack comes to an end. Keep in mind that this book has been written based on the last updates of the Sahara project in OpenStack up to the Liberty release. Its trend to move quickly and achieve fast growth will bring more features in the next releases. Again, the OpenStack journey never ends.

Index

A

affinity
  about 108
  policies 109
anti-affinity
  defining 110-115
Apache Hadoop 2.x.x
  URL 40
Apache Spark 4
Apache Spark plugin
  about 106
  image, building for 106, 107
  requirements and limitations 108
Apache Vanilla plugin
  image, building for 97-99
  requirements and limitations 100
architecture, Sahara
  components 12

B

big data
  big challenge 3
  defining 2
  dimensions 2
  moving to cloud, benefits 9
  revolution 3-5
  scalability problem, resolving 5
  use case, defining 5, 6
  Variety 2
  Velocity 2
  Volume 2

C

CDH high-availability support
  defining 133-139
CDH plugin
  about 102
  image, building for 103
  requirements and limitations 105, 106
CentOS 7
  URL 24
cinder-scheduler service 122
cinder-volume service 122
Command Line Interface (CLI) 31

D

Data Access Layer (DAL) 13
Database as a Service (DBaaS) 7
data processing
  cluster access, troubleshooting 154, 155
  cluster creation, troubleshooting 151
  cluster scaling, troubleshooting 153
  missing services, troubleshooting 151
  Sahara, debugging 148
  Sahara, logging 149, 150
  troubleshooting 147
  user quota, troubleshooting 152, 153
data reliability
  increasing 121-123
Disk Image Builder
  URL 97

K

Keystone 12
Kibana 151

L

Logstash and Kibana
reference 151

M

Mesos
URL 106
modes, SELinux
disabled 144
enforcing 144
permissive 144

N

network
defining 120, 121
Neutron networking component,
**   in OpenStack**
URL 19
Node Cluster Template
creating 54
creating, CLI used 57, 58
creating, with Horizon 55, 56
Node Group Template
creating 45
creating, CLI used 52-54
creating, in Horizon 45-51

O

OpenStack
about 6, 7
defining 141
identity, troubleshooting 145, 146
installing 15, 20
modules, defining 6, 7
networking, troubleshooting 146, 147
network requirements 20-22
OpenStack debug tool 142, 143

RDO installation, running 25-30
SELinux, troubleshooting 143-145
system requirements 23, 24
troubleshooting 141
URL 7
OpenStack all-in-one box
URL 26
OpenStack official community
URL 108
OpenStack Sahara
configuring 31-33
installing 31-33
OpenStack services
defining 12
OpenStack test networking layout
API network 18
Management network 17
Public network 17
VM network 18
OpenStack test topology environment
Cloud controller 16
Compute node 17
Network node 17
Storage nodes 17
overprovisioining and overcommitment
URL 153

R

RHadoop
about 5
URL 5

S

Sahara
about 15
architecture 12, 13
defining 8
in OpenStack 9, 10
integrating 31
Job binaries 64
Job glossary 63, 64
Jobs 65

Sahara OpenStack mission
  about 10, 11
  characteristics 10, 11
Sahara plugins
  affinity and anti-affinity 108-110
  Apache Spark plugin 106
  Cloudera Distribution Hadoop (CDH)
      plugin 102
  defining 96, 97
  Hortonworks Data Platform
      (HDP) plugin 100
  Vanilla Apache Hadoop 97
Sahara REST API
  URL 75
Sahara user interface
  installing 33-35
Savanna 9
SELinux
  URL 143
Simple Storage Service (S3)
  about 5
  URL 5
single point of failure (SPOF) 127
StandBy ResourceManager 133
Swift 9

T

test infrastructure environment
  OpenStack test environment design 18, 19
  OpenStack test networking layout 17, 18
  OpenStack test topology
      environment 16, 17
  preparing 16

tools, Hadoop project
  Ambari 4
  Avro 4
  Flume 4
  Hadoop 4
  HBase 4
  Hive 4
  Hue 4
  Mahout 4
  MapReduce 4
  Pig 4
  Storm 4
  Yarn 4
  ZooKeeper 4

V

Vanilla Apache Hadoop 97
vSphere 125

Y

YARN (Yet Another Resource
    Negotiator) 39

Z

ZKFC (Zookeeper Failover Controllers) 127

www.ingramcontent.com/pod-product-compliance
Lightning Source LLC
Chambersburg PA
CBHW060135060326
40690CB00018B/3891